CARDBOARD BOX
ENGINEERING

COOL, INVENTIVE PROJECTS
For Tinkerers, Makers & Future Scientists

Jonathan Adolph

Storey Publishing

For all the engineers of tomorrow
who are kids building with cardboard today

The mission of Storey Publishing is to serve our customers by
publishing practical information that encourages
personal independence in harmony with the environment.

Edited by Deanna F. Cook and Nancy Ringer

Art direction and book design by Jessica Armstrong

Text production and project styling by Liseann Karandisecky

Indexed by Christine R. Lindemer, Boston Road
Communications

Cover photography by Mars Vilaubi, © Storey Publishing,
except for © airdone/stock.adobe.com, front (tape); © Jakub
Krechowicz/Shutterstock.com, front (hole in box background);
Jessica Armstrong, © Storey Publishing, front (airplane);
© kolazig/stock.adobe.com, front (box)

Interior photography by Mars Vilaubi, © Storey Publishing

Additional interior photography by © 2020 Artists Rights
Society (ARS), New York, c/o Pictoright Amsterdam, 135 b.;
© acrogame/stock.adobe.com, 86 b.; © airdone/stock.adobe
.com, 23 and throughout (tape); © Aneese/stock.adobe.com,
99 t.; © Axel Koester/Getty Images, 29 b.; © Classic Image
/Alamy Stock Photo, 46 b.; © Dennis Hallinan/Alamy Stock
Photo, 61 b.; © FLHC 1B/Alamy Stock Photo, 16 m.r.; Jessica
Armstrong, © Storey Publishing, 1; © johnmerlin/stock.adobe
.com, 140 b.l.; © Jonathan Lingel/Dreamstime.com, 140 b.r.;
© kolazig/stock.adobe.com, 7 and throughout (empty box);
Courtesy of the Library of Congress, 46 t.; © Martin Rickett - PA
Images/Getty Images, 83 b.; © Michael Branscom for Lemelson
MIT, 102 b.; NASA, 9; © photka/iStock.com, 42 b.l.; Private
Collection © Look and Learn/Bridgeman Images, 33 b.; © Rafa
Irusta/stock.adobe.com, 140 b.c.; © RGB Ventures/SuperStock
/ Alamy Stock Photo, 16 t.r.; Artwork Copyright © and TM Rube
Goldberg Inc. All Rights Reserved. RUBE GOLDBERG® is a
registered trademark of Rube Goldberg Inc. All materials used
with permission. rubegoldberg.com, 146; © Science History
Images/Alamy Stock Photo, 16 b.l., 83 t.; © Siraphatphoto
/stock.adobe.com, 42 b.c.; © Stocksnapper/stock.adobe
.com, 29 and throughout (background); © Teen00000/iStock
.com, 121; © The Print Collector/Alamy Stock Photo, 16 m.l.;
© YOSHIKAZU TSUNO/Getty Images, 144 b.; Rights Held by
Ypsilanti Historical Society/Creative Commons Attribution-
Share Alike 4.0 International, 116 b.; © ZUMA Press, Inc./Alamy
Stock Photo, 164 b.

Illustrations and diagrams by Ian O'Neill, © Storey Publishing

Text © 2020 by Jonathan Adolph

Storey books are available at special discounts when purchased in bulk for
premiums and sales promotions as well as for fund-raising or educational use.
Special editions or book excerpts can also be created to specification. For
details, please call 800-827-8673, or send an email to sales@storey.com.

Storey Publishing
210 MASS MoCA Way
North Adams, MA 01247
storey.com

Printed in China through Asia Pacific Offset
10 9 8 7 6 5 4 3 2

Library of Congress Cataloging-in-Publication Data

Names: Adolph, Jonathan, author.
Title: Cardboard box engineering : cool, inventive projects for tinkerers,
   makers & future scientists / Jonathan Adolph.
Description: North Adams, MA : Storey Publishing, [2020] | Includes index.
   | Audience: Ages 9–14 | Audience: Grades 4–6
Identifiers: LCCN 2020030019 (print) | LCCN 2020030020 (ebook)
   | ISBN 9781635862140 (paperback) | ISBN 9781635863604 (hardcover)
   | ISBN 9781635862157 (ebook)
Subjects: LCSH: Box craft—Juvenile literature. | Cardboard art—Juvenile
   literature. | Science—Experiments—Juvenile literature.
Classification: LCC TT870.5 .A36 2020 (print) | LCC TT870.5 (ebook)
   | DDC 745.54—dc23
LC record available at https://lccn.loc.gov/2020030019
LC ebook record available at https://lccn.loc.gov/2020030020

CONTENTS

CHAPTER 4
BUILT TO MOVE
AERONAUTICS & NAUTICAL ENGINEERING

CHAPTER 5
ELEGANT DESIGN
MECHANICAL ENGINEERING

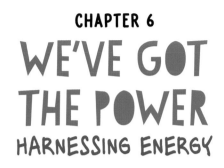

CHAPTER 6
WE'VE GOT THE POWER
HARNESSING ENERGY

CHAPTER 7
SERIOUS FUN
GAME DESIGN

CHAPTER 1

THE SCIENCE OF ENGINEERING

Of all the creatures that have ever lived on this planet, we modern humans are the champions of making stuff. I know, I know: beavers build dams, honeybees create honeycombs, birds make nests, and spiders spin webs. Those are all very impressive, especially when you don't have thumbs! But none of that really compares to what people produce today, and if you doubt me, just ask your mobile phone as you are flying in a jet over a skyscraper. We've invented a few things that have caused us problems (I'm looking at you, atomic bomb!), but far more often, we come up with marvels of engineering that change our lives for the better.

Why is that? What allows people to be so good at building things?

In a word: science. We humans have science, the greatest tool ever invented for figuring out how things work, and how they could be made to work better. Thanks to the scientific method — the process of making predictions and then testing them — we can try out our ideas and separate the good from the bad. Science is what gives engineers and designers the knowledge to produce all the amazing devices that surround us — including every toy, game, and electronic gizmo you own.

And here's the best part: You can be one of those people. You can be a designer and an engineer. With the help of this book, you'll learn how to turn old boxes, cartons, tubes, and other cardboard into games, airplanes, robots, roller coasters, and more. And, in the process, you'll see what engineering and design are all about.

WHY CARDBOARD?

To learn how to do anything right, you need to practice. And to practice engineering, you need stuff that can be engineered. That's where cardboard comes in.

Cardboard is an amazing invention in its own right. It's easy to cut and assemble, but it's also sturdy and durable. Even better, it's free.

You probably have a pile of it lying around your house right now: mailing boxes stacked in the basement, cereal boxes and cardboard tubes filling the recycling bin. That means you may already have what you need to start making stuff, and maybe even enough to make a project several times.

And that's important, because engineers know that projects rarely work perfectly the first time. In fact, the best engineers love to make things over and over because each time they do, they get a chance to improve the design. They start by building an experimental model, called a *prototype*, and then improve it using the scientific method — they test the model, see if it works as expected, tinker with it if it

Almost everything you buy travels by cardboard box — 95 percent of all products in the United States, to be exact. That requires about 30 million tons of boxes each year.

Many corrugated cardboard boxes used for shipping have a stamp that gives their rating in an "edge crush test," a measure of how strong they are. Look for it on the bottom of the box.

doesn't, and then test it again. Whenever something doesn't work out, they've learned something new.

As the great engineer and inventor Thomas Edison said, "When I have eliminated the ways that will not work, I will find the way that will work."

The cardboard projects in this book let you do just this kind of tinkering. They're engineered in a particular way, but other options might be just as interesting. For each project, think about what you are trying to build, how it is supposed to work, and how you might be able to make it work even better. If you hit a snag, be like Thomas Edison and try something else. You might need to substitute a new material for one you don't have or come up with another way to attach two parts. Make adjustments, change the design, test out new ideas, be creative.

Do that, and you'll be learning more than how to build with cardboard. You'll be learning how to build with *any* material. Because the process of engineering is the same no matter what you are tinkering with, and all engineering is based on the same laws: the laws of science.

WORKING THE PROBLEM

In the movie *Apollo 13*, there's a scene that demonstrates engineering in its purest form. The team at Mission Control has just discovered a problem with the carbon dioxide filters in the damaged spacecraft, and the astronauts need to fix it or they will die. Back on Earth, the engineers head to their lab and collect objects similar to what's on the spacecraft. "Listen up," says the lead engineer. "We gotta find a way to make this" — he holds up a square filter — "fit into the hole for this" — he holds up a round one — "using nothing but that" — and he points to the pile of stuff on the table. (Spoiler alert: They do it.)

Those engineers helped save that 1970 moon mission, but you don't have to be a rocket scientist to solve problems through engineering. In our everyday lives, we are all constantly "working the problem," as the Mission Control engineers put it, whether it's trying to get a chain back on a bike gear, assembling a new toy, or finding a way to fit all your stuff in your backpack. Engineering is about understanding how stuff works, and then using that knowledge to build other stuff that works or to fix things that have stopped working. As *Apollo 13* showed us, the results can be out of this world.

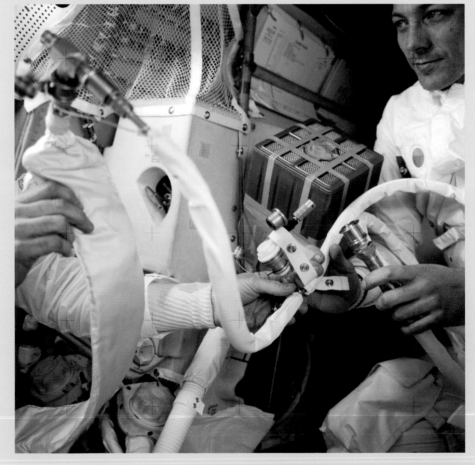

Apollo 13 astronaut John L. Swigert Jr. shows how the crew "worked the problem" on the troubled spacecraft.

KNOW YOUR CARDBOARD

Many different materials go by the name *cardboard*. All are made from a mash of ground-up wood or paper, but they differ in appearance, strength, and texture. To a cardboard engineer, each type is valuable, so start collecting supplies of the following kinds.

CORRUGATED CARDBOARD. This extra-thick box material, technically called *corrugated fiberboard*, is what probably comes first to mind when you hear the word *cardboard*. The sandwich of layers makes it particularly sturdy. But even corrugated cardboard is not all the same: there's singlewall (one inner layer), doublewall (two layers), and even the rare triplewall (three layers!). This is the stuff to use whenever you need a stiff and durable material for a project.

SINGLEWALL

The waves of paper are called *flutes*.

DOUBLEWALL

The sturdy outer paper is called *linerboard*.

Corrugated cardboard is categorized by the size of the flutes, either A, B, C (the most common), E, or F. Weirdly, that order is based on when the size was invented, not which is bigger.

PAPERBOARD. Cartons that hold cereal, crackers, cookies, and other dry foods, as well as shoe boxes and file folders, are made from paperboard (also called chipboard), a type of single-layer cardboard. The outside of a paperboard carton is often glossy with ink, while the inside is usually a flat grayish tan. Frozen foods are often sold in paperboard boxes that have smooth white inside surfaces. Paperboard is easier to cut than corrugated cardboard, and it's flexible, so it's easy to roll and fold.

PLASTIC-COATED PAPERBOARD. Cartons that hold milk, orange juice, and other liquids are made from paperboard coated with a thin layer of plastic and sealed with heat to make them waterproof. Aseptic containers — the flat-topped cartons that hold juice, soy milk, soups, and other liquids at room temperature — are also made from coated paperboard, but with an additional layer of aluminum foil that keeps the food inside the cartons from going bad.

TUBES. Like boxes, cardboard tubes come in all sizes and strengths, from narrow drinking straws to wider toilet paper and paper towel tubes and longer wrapping paper and mailing tubes. You can use tubes for supports, cut them into rings, and slice them lengthwise into troughs.

In 2012, British skydiver Gary Connery jumped from a helicopter wearing a wingsuit and landed without a parachute on a 12-foot-high cushion built from nearly 20,000 cardboard boxes — an activity we did not attempt for this book!

MOLDED PULP CONTAINERS. Pulp is a paste-like mix of recycled paper fibers and water, sort of like papier-mâché. When it's molded, or formed, and allowed to dry, it becomes a stiff cardboard with surprising strength. Molded pulp containers such as egg cartons and heavy-duty paper plates offer interesting shapes for your cardboard engineering projects.

The cardboard box was inducted into the National Toy Hall of Fame in 2005, confirming what many people believe: it's often more fun to play with the box than the toy that came in it.

THE ART OF CUTTING

Cutting cardboard accurately, quickly, and safely requires the right tools for the job. In addition to a good pair of scissors, you'll need a small saw, a sharp knife, a straightedge, and a good surface to cut on.

1 **Scissors** are fine for cutting paperboard and trimming edges, but they can be hard to use for longer cuts in thick corrugated cardboard.

2 **Cuticle scissors** — small pointed scissors used to cut fingernails — are a good choice for precise trimming, especially with thin cardboard.

3 A **small saw** is good for making long cuts in corrugated cardboard and removing flaps from boxes. Any fine-toothed variety, such as a drywall saw or hacksaw, will work.

4 A **cardboard saw**, such as the Canary Cardboard Cutter, is specifically designed for cardboard. You'll find that it cuts easily, accurately, and safely — and it's inexpensive.

5 A **utility knife** with a locking blade cuts cardboard easily. Use it on a cutting mat with a straightedge for making clean, straight cuts.

6 A **craft knife** (such as an X-Acto) is a great cardboard cutting tool. You can use it with a straightedge on a cutting mat to make straight cuts, and you can also use it freehand to cut detailed shapes.

7 A **straightedge**, such as a ruler, can be used as a guide for making straight cuts. A metal ruler with a cork backing is best. It won't slip on your cardboard and won't be damaged by your knife blade.

MAKING THE CUT

CUT AWAY FROM YOUR FINGERS — and any other body parts that you care about.

CHANGE YOUR BLADE WHEN IT GETS DULL. A sharp knife is dangerous, but a dull one that sticks or slips is worse.

TAKE YOUR TIME. Rather than trying to cut through thick cardboard with one deep pass, make several careful passes with your knife. It's safer and less likely to lead to mistakes.

A NONSLIP CORK-BACKED RULER works well as a guide for straight cuts.

WHEN USING A SAW, hold the cardboard on your work table with the cut line parallel and close to the edge of the table for support.

A CUTTING MAT protects your work surface, and since the knife can't dig into the mat, the cutting is smoother and safer.

PUTTING IT ALL TOGETHER

When you're building with cardboard, the right glue, tape, or fastener can make the difference between fun and frustration.

LOW-TEMPERATURE HOT GLUE. Hot glue is used with a plug-in "gun." It is the go-to glue for most of the projects in this book, and for good reason. The guns and glue sticks don't cost that much, the melted glue bonds almost immediately, and the glue's gooey consistency adds support and fills gaps. The downsides: it's hot (duh!), it bonds so quickly that you don't have much time to reposition pieces, and it doesn't hold paint.

WHITE GLUES. Common craft glues (such as Tacky Glue and Elmer's) work well with cardboard, but they usually require that you hold or clamp the pieces until the glue sets. On the plus side, the longer drying time means that you can reposition pieces after you've glued them to get them just right.

GLUE STICKS. These paste sticks work well for attaching layers of paper, but they aren't strong enough to hold anything under pressure.

MASKING TAPE. This everyday stand-by is an excellent choice for cardboard. It's reasonably strong, bonds well, and is easy to tear. The downside: it can look a bit drab. Blue painter's tape is a more colorful alternative. It's also less tacky, which makes it easier to reposition.

CLEAR PACKING TAPE. Made for sealing cardboard boxes, this inexpensive tape is almost invisible and quite strong, especially for reinforcing seams and hinges. It's far better than ordinary cellophane tape (such as Scotch tape), which often doesn't hold up. Once it's in place, however, it will tear the cardboard if you try to remove it.

DUCT TAPE. This cloth-based tape is handy when you need even more strength and where thickness is not an issue. A layer of duct tape can also give cardboard a durable coating, and colored tapes can provide decoration. But it's harder to tear than masking tape and a bit fussy to cut.

CLOTHESPINS. Spring clothespins are handy fasteners for joining pieces that needs to be taken apart now and then. They can also serve as clamps when you're using white glue.

PAPER FASTENERS. These metal pins with bendable tabs provide a quick, easy, and mess-free way to join cardboard piees. They can even allow those cardboard pieces to rotate if you make holes for the fasteners. The downside: they are not very strong and can pull out over time.

There's no better glue for cardboard construction than hot glue, but keep in mind: it's called hot glue for a reason! Load a stick of glue into the gun, squeeze the trigger, and the glue gets pressed through a hole in the tip and oozes out like hot gooey toothpaste. As the melted glue cools, it hardens, quickly bonding to whatever it's touching. As magical as hot glue can be, keep these safety tips in mind:

* *After you plug it in, let the gun fully warm up* (depending on the model, this can take as long as 10 minutes). The gun is ready to use when the glue squeezes out easily.

* *When you're not using it,* set the glue gun on a nonflammable surface, like an old dinner plate, a ceramic tile, or a square of aluminum foil. Most guns are designed to stand on their end, with the tip safely in the air.

* *When applying glue, keep the gun's tip as close to the project as possible.* Squeeze out a line of glue, then twist the gun as you pull it away. This helps avoid creating long, stringy strands of glue.

* *Hold the glued pieces together for at least a count of ten* so the glue can set (it will still be hot!).

* *To remove a blob of glue* that's gotten somewhere you don't want, wait until it cools, then peel it off.

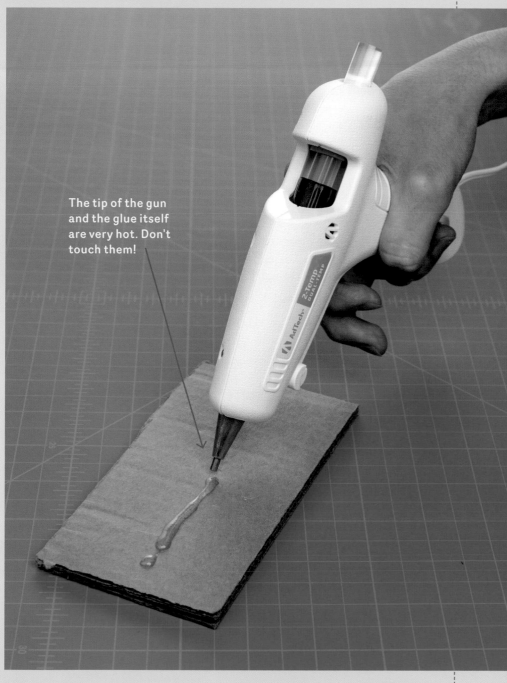

The tip of the gun and the glue itself are very hot. Don't touch them!

* *Have lots of glue sticks on hand* (you'll go through them quickly). Make sure that they are the right kind and size for your gun.

* *Unplug the gun when you are finished.* If the gun's tip is messy, you — or an adult, if you're feeling nervous about getting burned — can clean it by twisting it in a wad of aluminum foil while it is still warm.

PLANS, DIAGRAMS, AND DRAWINGS

Engineers and designers use drawings to plan their projects, to show others how the pieces go together, and to help bring an idea to life. These drawings might be architectural blueprints, electrical diagrams, computer-generated models, or just a sketch on a scrap of paper. Diagrams are the language of engineering and design because when you are trying to build something, a picture really is worth a thousand words.

Many of the projects in this book use diagrams, as well as photographs and words, to explain how the parts go together. Be sure to look them over carefully so you understand what they are telling you. Learning how to speak the language of diagrams is a skill every engineer needs to know.

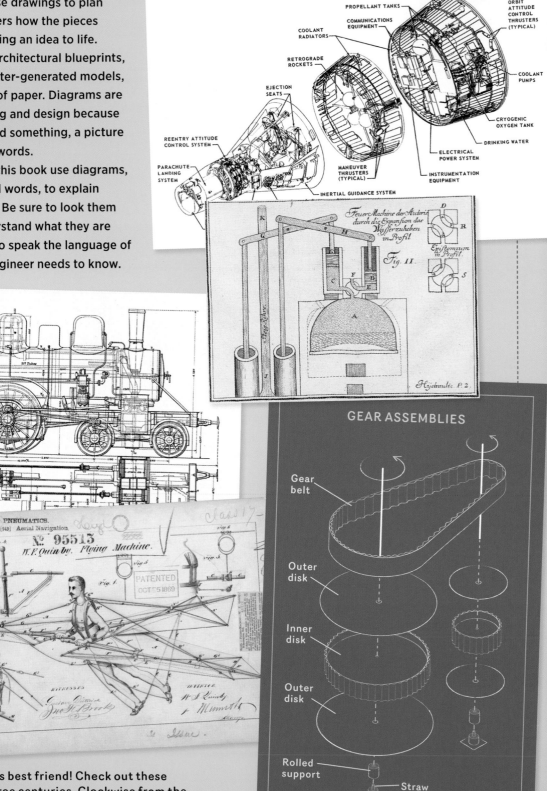

Diagrams are an engineer's best friend! Check out these examples from the last three centuries. Clockwise from the top: a 1966 diagram of NASA's *Gemini* rocket, a steam engine designed in 1720 by German engineer Jacob Leupold, our very own Handmade Spin Art (page 106), an 1869 patent drawing for a flying machine, and a steam locomotive drawn in 1901.

TRICKS OF THE TRADE

The following engineering techniques are used throughout this book. Once you master them, you'll be able to assemble all kinds of cardboard creations.

TEMPLATE TRANSFER

We've provided drawing templates at the end of this book for some of the projects. There are a couple of ways to transfer these templates to cardboard, depending on the project.

NOTE: *If this is a library or school book, please don't cut out the templates! Trace them or make photocopies to cut out.*

CUT OUT AND TRACE: For simpler designs, cut out the shape that's marked on the paper template. Then, holding the cut-out template in place, trace around it on your cardboard. You'll use this technique for the Swinging Monkey on page 40 and the Floating Hummingbird on page 90.

GLUE AND CUT OUT: Glue the paper template onto the cardboard and then cut around the marked shape. This technique is used for project templates, like the Three-Wing Boomerang on page 62 and the Wind-Powered Tractor on page 130.

ROLL A BEARING

By tightly rolling a strip of corrugated cardboard around a straw, you can make a log-like cylinder that works as a bearing — a device that holds an axle while allowing it to turn. You can use the same technique to add a solid handle to a skewer or dowel. By changing how you glue the strip of cardboard, you can make a sturdy cardboard sleeve with lots of uses.

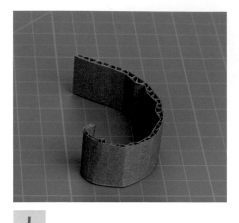

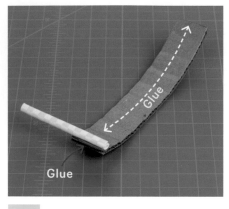

1 To prepare the cardboard strip for a tight roll, it helps to preroll it: roll the strip around a skewer, dowel, or pencil to form it into a cylinder. Then unroll it.

2 Hot-glue the straw to the leading edge of the cardboard strip. Then apply a line of glue down the length of the cardboard.

3 Tightly roll the strip back up.

Or Roll a Handle or Support

You can use the same technique to add a solid handle or support cylinder to a skewer or dowel.

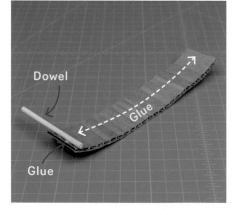

Or Roll a Sleeve

If you roll the cardboard around the dowel but *don't* glue the dowel in place, you can make a sleeve.

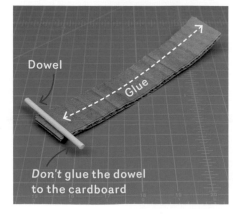

DRAW A CIRCLE

The circle is a key shape in engineering, allowing such momentous inventions as the wheel, the pulley, and, of course, the Frisbee. To cut a circle from cardboard, you first need to draw one. Here are a few techniques.

TRACE: The easiest method is to simply find a circular object of the right size — a plate, a cup, even a coin — and trace around it.

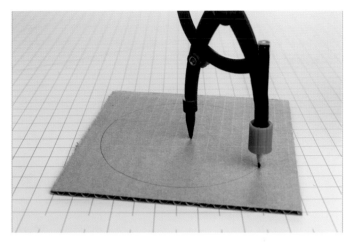

USE A COMPASS: To draw a circle with a center point (which is handy for making an axle hole for wheels), use a compass. Adjust the legs to set the circle's size, stick the point in your cardboard, and rotate the pencil point around the center to draw a perfect ring.

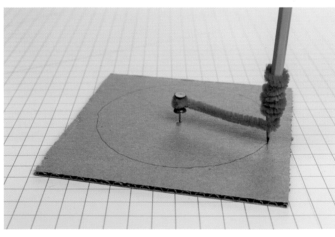

MAKE A COMPASS: If you don't have a compass handy, you can use a pipe cleaner with one end twisted around a pencil and the other twisted around a pushpin. Press the pushpin into the cardboard, pull the pipe cleaner taut, and draw your circle with the pencil.

MAKE A TEMPLATE: If you need to make several identical circles, draw and cut one, then trace around it to make the rest. If you need to mark the center point on all of these circles, draw the first circle with a compass, which will mark its center point. One by one, stack the first circle on top of the others and poke a pushpin through that center point into the circle below.

CREASING AND FOLDING

Thick cardboard can be hard to fold. Creasing it first produces a clean straight edge.

  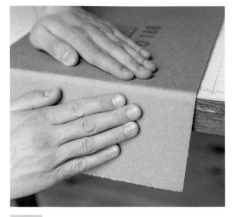

1 Using a pencil and a straightedge, draw a line where you want to fold the cardboard.

2 Using your straightedge as a guide, press down along that line with a popsicle stick, a knitting needle, or a similar tool, flattening the top layer of the cardboard's linerboard. Now you've creased the cardboard.

3 Turn the cardboard upside down and align the crease with the edge of your work table. Fold the cardboard down along the crease line. For a narrower piece of cardboard, place a ruler along the crease line and fold the cardboard up (see page 49).

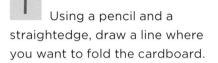

SCORING: With thick cardboard, you can create a sharper edge by scoring the fold rather than creasing it. Using a straightedge and a knife, carefully slice through just the top linerboard, then bend the cardboard so it hinges on the remaining layers. The resulting fold is weaker, so consider reinforcing it with tape.

PEELING CORRUGATED CARDBOARD

Peeling the linerboard from a piece of corrugated cardboard exposes the flutes, allowing you to bend and curve the cardboard into airplane wings, gear belts, tire treads, and more.

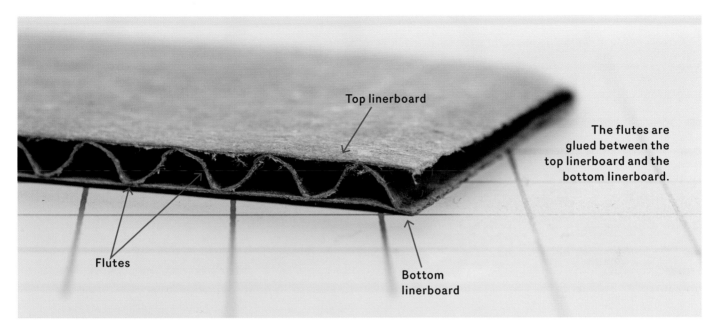

Top linerboard

The flutes are glued between the top linerboard and the bottom linerboard.

Flutes

Bottom linerboard

1 Cut the cardboard to the size you need. Using the tip of a pencil or skewer, separate the top linerboard from the first flute, peeling back enough linerboard so that you can grab it with your fingers.

NOTE: Some projects in this book require the flutes in the cardboard to run in a certain direction, so check the instructions before you cut the cardboard.

2 Peel away the linerboard, working one flute at a time so the pieces separate cleanly. When you're done, if any bits of linerboard remain stuck on the flutes, gently pry them off.

PUSHPIN PUNCTURE

This technique lets you make holes in cardboard for dowels, toothpicks, wires, straws, and more. It even works for poking holes in thin plastic, such as milk carton caps.

As you push the pushpin and other sharp tools through the cardboard, be careful not to accidentally puncture your hand on the other side!

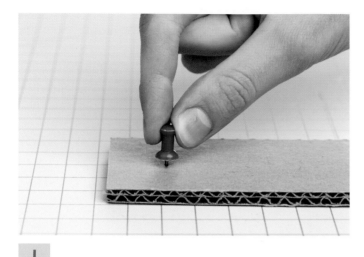

1 Mark where you want your hole. Start the hole by pushing a pushpin through the spot you just marked. Give it a few twists.

2 Remove the pushpin and insert a toothpick, giving it a few twists as well.

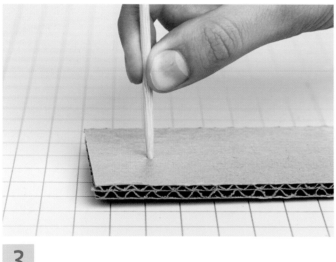

3 For a bigger hole, insert a skewer and twist that.

4 If you need an even bigger hole, twist in a pencil.

CHAPTER 2

MECHANICAL MARVELS

ROBOTICS & ANIMATRONICS

The field of robotics has given us amazing devices that do things humans don't want to do (thank you, floor-sweeping Roomba!) or can't do as well, or as quickly, as a machine. If you want to assemble a car, defuse a bomb, explore a shipwreck, or perform delicate surgery, a robot can be a huge help.

The history of robotics goes back centuries. The earliest inventors and engineers often tried to create machines that acted like living things to amuse or impress others. We still love to be entertained by robots, as R2D2, Wall-E, and the many other mechanical movie stars attest. In fact, there's a whole field of engineering called animatronics (a word that combines *animate* and *electronics*) that's all about using robotic science at theme parks and in movies. The robin that sings in the 1964 movie *Mary Poppins* was one of the first examples. Other animatronic favorites: the shark in *Jaws*, E.T., the dinosaurs in *Jurassic Park*, and the Hall of Presidents at Walt Disney World. Learn how engineers bring machines to life in the projects that follow.

EXTENDING GRABBER

These long-reaching hands are built from interconnected levers that open and close like scissors, allowing you to, say, pick up stinky socks from a safe distance. Use the most durable cardboard you can find for your levers; doublewall corrugated cardboard works well.

This design uses four levers that can be as long as 2 feet each, but you might try connecting additional pairs of shorter levers for a more accordion-style grabber, like the one shown at bottom right.

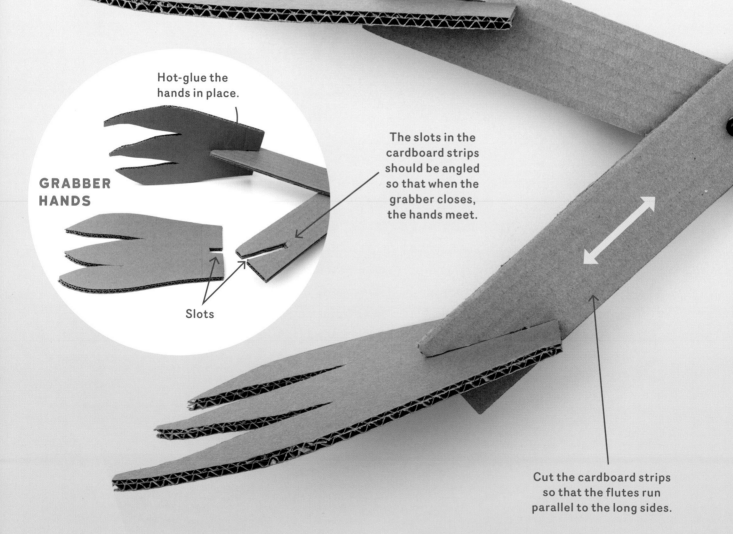

Hot-glue the hands in place.

GRABBER HANDS

Slots

The slots in the cardboard strips should be angled so that when the grabber closes, the hands meet.

Cut the cardboard strips so that the flutes run parallel to the long sides.

TOOTHPICK PIN

Be sure you can put the toothpick through the beads. Hot-glue wooden beads in place on both sides.

Round wooden toothpick

If you like, wrap the ends of the handles with duct tape for a better grip.

After the glue dries, snip off the ends of the toothpick so they're flush with the beads.

Pin the cardboard strips at their center and 1 inch in from their ends.

1"

Take It Further

Your grabbers can be more than just handy. Get creative and turn them into grippy lizard feet or something toothy, like shark jaws. You can attach them to the levers with paper fasteners instead of toothpick pins.

You can also use paper fasteners to pin the joints.

ROBOTIC HAND

The human hand is marvel of engineering, capable of powerfully lifting a climber up a mountain face, precisely threading a needle, or gracefully playing the violin. Engineers have long sought to create robotic hands with similar dexterity, and many of their designs are truly remarkable. This one — controlled by your hand in a glove — won't let you perform surgery or assemble a computer, but it will let you wiggle your new giant fingers, make the peace sign, and give a big robotic thumbs-up.

To point your robotic finger here . . .

SPEAK LIKE AN ENGINEER

Biomimetics or *biomimicry* is the process of basing a design on something found in nature. The strings in this robotic hand, for example, mimic the tendons found in our actual hands. If a design involves more technology, engineers might call it *bionic*, a term made popular by the 1970s television show *The Six Million Dollar Man*, about the world's first bionic human. (These days, of course, six million dollars might get you only a bionic hand!)

honey nut hoops

. . . just do the same in here!

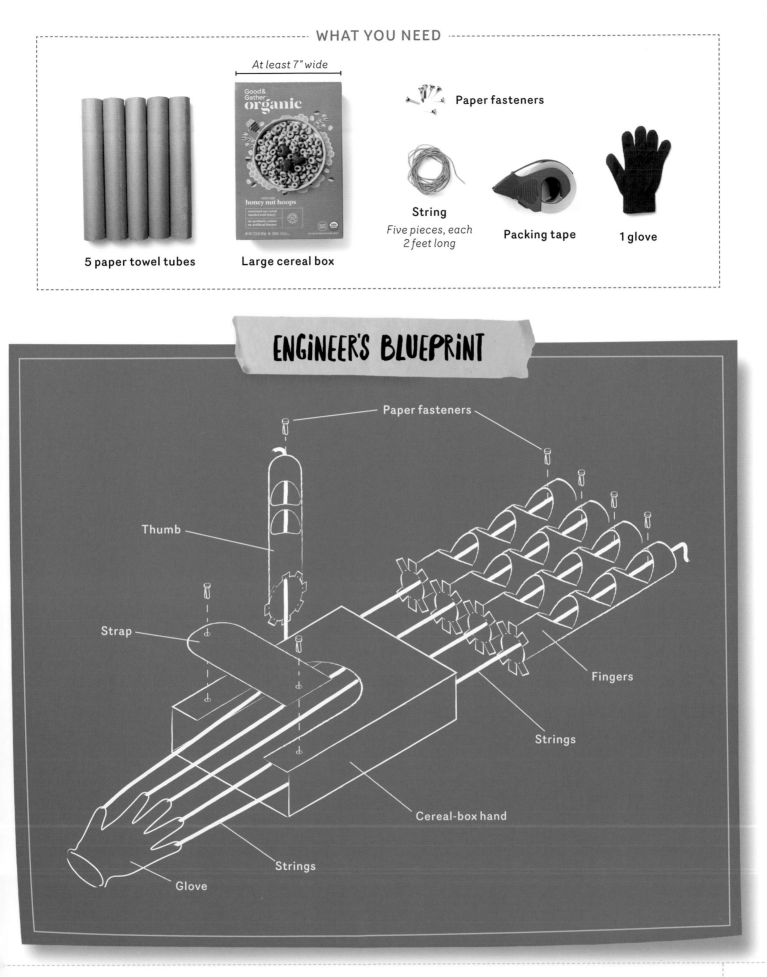

At least 7" wide

Good & Gather
organic

honey nut hoops

5 paper towel tubes

Large cereal box

Paper fasteners

String
Five pieces, each 2 feet long

Packing tape

1 glove

ENGINEER'S BLUEPRINT

Paper fasteners

Thumb

Strap

Fingers

Strings

Cereal-box hand

Strings

Glove

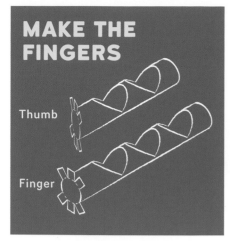

MAKE THE FINGERS

Thumb

Finger

NOTE: The finger joints are diamond-shaped holes cut into the cardboard tubes. The four fingers each have three holes, while the thumb has two holes.

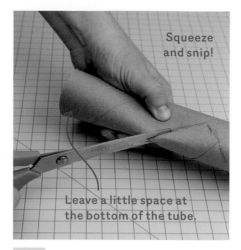

Squeeze and snip!

Leave a little space at the bottom of the tube.

1 Use a pencil to mark the diamond-shaped "joints" evenly down the tubes, leaving a little extra space at the bottom. Then cut out those diamond shapes, gently squeezing the tubes and snipping across the fold.

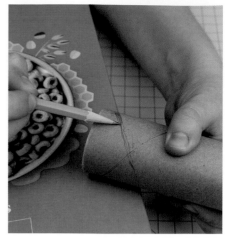

2 Hold the thumb tube against the side of the cereal box at an angle, as shown — just like your thumb is set at an angle on your hand. Use a pencil to mark the angle where the tube meets the box. Trim the bottom of the tube along that angled line.

3 Snip the bottoms of the tubes to make small tabs. Fold the tabs upward.

4 Apply packing tape to the fronts and backs of the tubes, working around the diamond-shaped holes, to reinforce them.

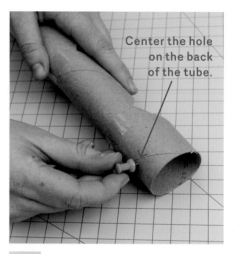

Center the hole on the back of the tube.

5 Use a pushpin to poke a hole through the top of each tube, on the back side. Wiggle it around to make the hole big enough for a paper fastener.

PREPARE THE BOX

Cut a large opening here.

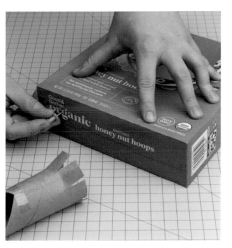

6 Remove the flaps from the opened end of the cereal box. Cut a large opening in the front panel, as shown. (Save the piece you cut out for the strap you'll make later.)

7 Using a pushpin and one of the cardboard finger tubes as a guide, make four evenly spaced holes across the unopened end of the box. Make another hole on the side for the thumb. Use the Pushpin Puncture technique (page 22) to make the holes big enough for your string.

ENGINEER SPOTLIGHT: CHRISTIAN RISTOW

New Mexico engineer and artist Christian Ristow (born in 1970) took the idea of a mechanical hand to the robotic extreme with his interactive sculpture *Hand of Man,* a popular attraction at festivals and Maker Faires since its debut in 2008. Made of metal, 26 feet long, and powered by hydraulics, it's capable of picking up and crushing cars. It, too, is operated by a glove-like controller, and members of the audience are allowed to try it for themselves. Search for "Ristow's Hand of Man" on YouTube to see the device in action.

FLYING PTERODACTYL

This flying reptile is an example of an *automaton*, a type of robotic sculpture that engineers and artists have been making for hundreds of years (search online for "automata sculptures" and prepare to be amazed!). The key mechanical element here is a turning wire, called a *crankshaft*, whose bent tabs, called *cams*, transform the crank's spinning motion into the up-and-down motion of the pterodactyl's wings.

Pterodactyls not your cup of "ptea"? For other automaton ideas, see page 35.

Turn the crankshaft to make the pterodactyl fly!

One mechanical sculpture is an *automaton*.

Two or more are *automata*.

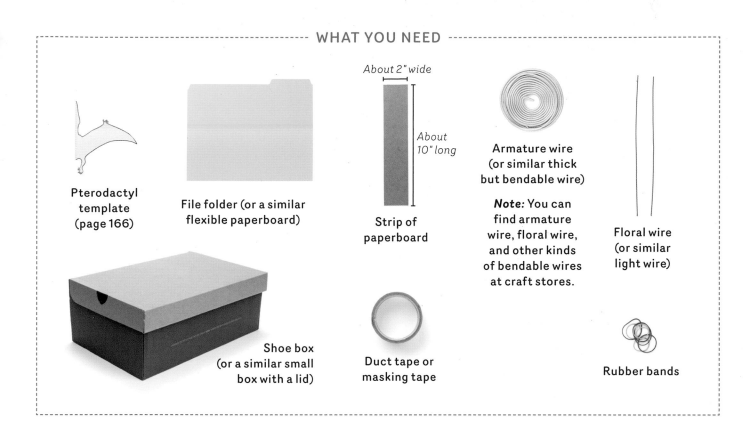

Pterodactyl template (page 166)

File folder (or a similar flexible paperboard)

About 2" wide

About 10" long

Strip of paperboard

Armature wire (or similar thick but bendable wire)

Note: You can find armature wire, floral wire, and other kinds of bendable wires at craft stores.

Floral wire (or similar light wire)

Shoe box (or a similar small box with a lid)

Duct tape or masking tape

Rubber bands

ENGINEER SPOTLIGHT: JACQUES DE VAUCANSON

Over the centuries, artists and engineers have created amazing automata that imitate living things, perform complicated movements, and even tell stories. One of the most remarkable was the *Digesting Duck*, built in 1739 by inventor and engineer Jacques de Vaucanson (1709–1782), who, being French, called it *Le Canard Digérateur*. This life-size mechanical bird made of gold-plated copper could not only quack and move like a duck but also eat and drink — and then poop! Despite its name (and Vaucanson's claims), the duck did not actually digest food. The poop that came out was fake. But the *Digesting Duck* still amazed those who saw it, and in the process of engineering its artificial intestines, Vaucanson invented the world's first rubber tube.

The *Digesting Duck*'s creator, as imagined by an artist in the 1800s.

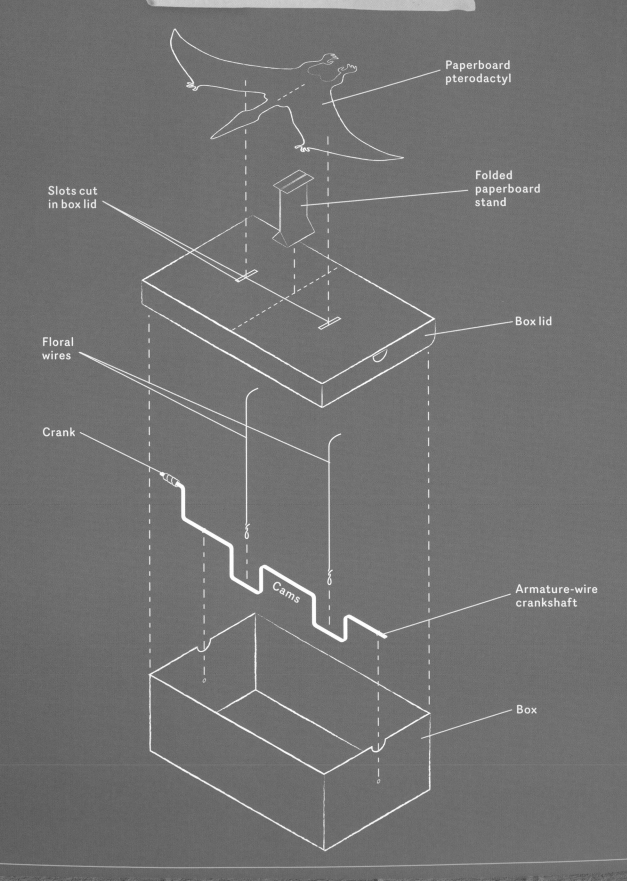

Paperboard pterodactyl

Folded paperboard stand

Slots cut in box lid

Box lid

Floral wires

Crank

Cams

Armature-wire crankshaft

Box

MAKE THE STAND AND PTERODACTYL

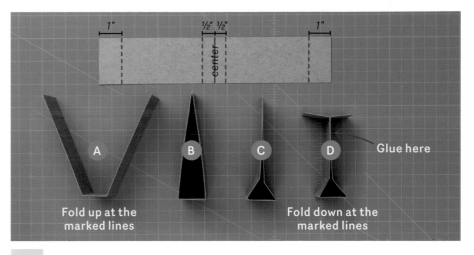

1"   ½" ½"   1"

center

A   B   C   D   Glue here

Fold up at the marked lines   Fold down at the marked lines

1 Measure and mark the strip of paperboard, and then fold and hot-glue a stand, as shown.

2 Tape the template on the folded edge of a file folder. Trace around the template. Then remove the template and cut out the pterodactyl.

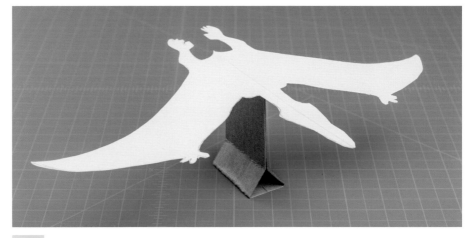

3 Hot-glue the pterodactyl to the stand.

Take It Further

Using the same mechanism (and the templates on pages 166–167), you can make a soaring eagle, a flapping bat, and a fluttering luna moth — or design something else that would be fun to see moving. For a more dramatic rocking action, like a ship tossing on waves, bend one cam down and the other up, and mount the automaton sideways.

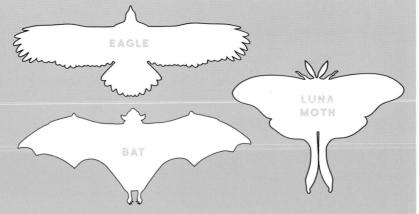

EAGLE

LUNA MOTH

BAT

PREPARE THE BOX

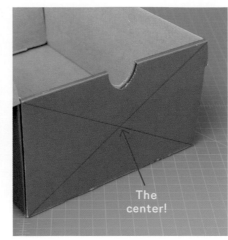

The center!

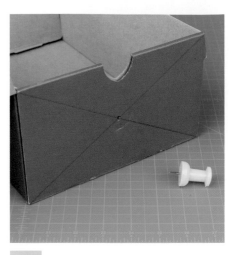

4 Using a ruler and a pencil, draw lines diagonally across each end of the box, from corner to corner. The point where the two lines cross is the center. (This trick works for finding the center of any rectangle!)

5 Using a pushpin, poke a hole at the center point on each end of the box. Using the Pushpin Puncture technique (page 22), make the holes large enough to fit the armature wire.

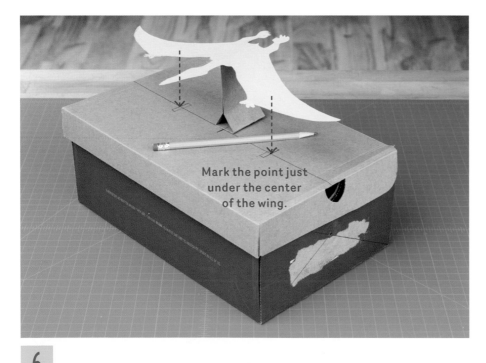

Mark the point just under the center of the wing.

6 Measure and mark a line across the middle of the box top. Then mark the center of that line. Set the pterodactyl on the center point. On the line across the top of the box, mark a spot on either side of the pterodactyl that is at about the midpoint of the wings.

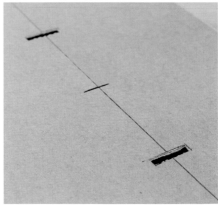

7 Mark and cut slots at those two points, as shown. Our slots are about 1 inch long and ¼ inch wide.

INSTALL THE CRANKSHAFT

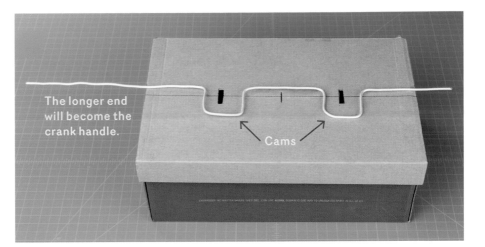

The longer end will become the crank handle.

Cams

8 With wire cutters, cut a length of armature wire about twice as long as your box. This will become the crankshaft. Bend two cams along the wire, aligning them with the slots in the top of the box. Leave enough wire on one end to make the crank handle.

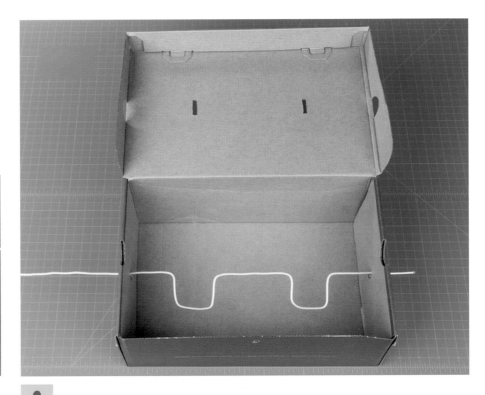

Center point

NOTE: Check the depth of your cams by laying the wire across the center point you marked on the end of the box. The cams shouldn't reach the bottom of the box. If they do, they'll hit the bottom or top of the box when you turn the crank.

9 Feed the longer handle end of the crankshaft from inside the box out one of the holes at the end of the box. Then feed the other end through the hole at the opposite end of the box. (If you need to bend the wire in order to do this, go ahead! Just straighten it out again afterward.) Adjust the wire as necessary so that the cams are in place under the slots.

We used a rubber band to secure our crankshaft, but you could also use tape.

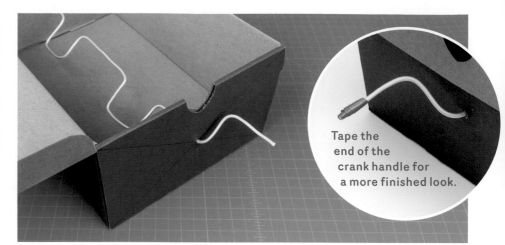

Tape the end of the crank handle for a more finished look.

10 On the opposite end of the box, wrap a rubber band around the wire where it exits the box to hold it in place. Then trim it, if needed.

11 For the handle, bend a crank shape on the end of the wire, and trim off any extra.

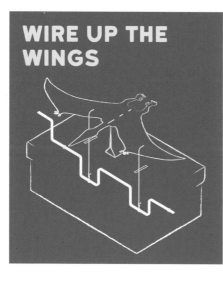

WIRE UP THE WINGS

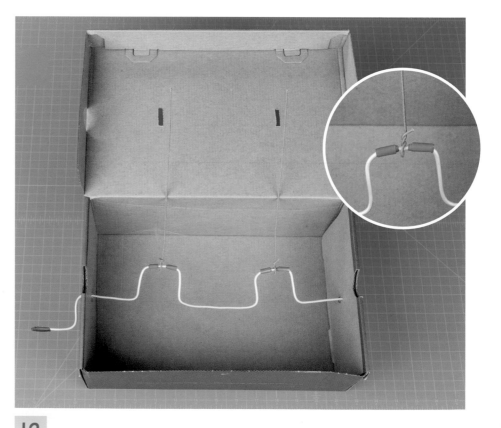

12 Cut two lengths of floral wire, about 10 inches each. Wrap one end of each wire around each cam. Wrap strips of tape on either side of the camshaft to keep the wire in place.

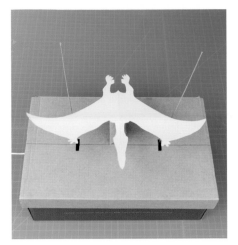

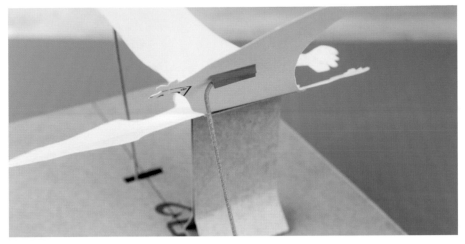

13   Feed the floral wires through the slots. Close the box. Hot-glue the pterodactyl and its stand in place on top of the box.

14   Now you'll have to tinker. Turn the crank handle. When the cams are turned upward, the wires should be pushing the wings up to their highest position. When you have the length right, bend the wires to make a tab at that length, and trim off any extra wire. Tape the wire tabs to the underside of the wings.

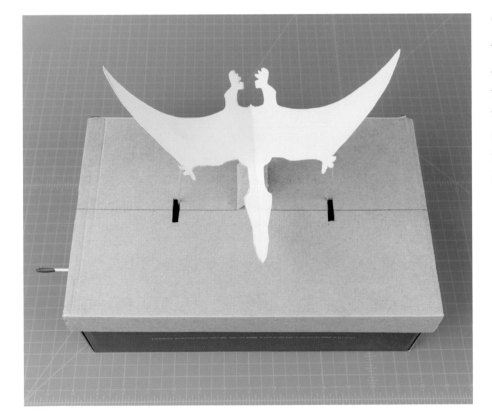

TEST AND TINKER

Test the mechanism by turning the crank handle and observing how the wings move. You may need to tinker with the wire lengths, the slots, where you've taped on the floral wire — whatever it takes to get your pterodactyl flying!

SWINGING MONKEY

This high-energy monkey is powered by the simplest of engineering tools: the lever. The cardboard crosspiece is key, serving as what engineers call the *fulcrum*. Squeezing the handles below the fulcrum causes the top ends of the levers to spread apart. That pulls the twisted strings, which starts the monkey spinning. Another squeeze sends him swinging back. The wooden bead spacers provide extra weight to improve the swinging action.

We chose a monkey for our swinging creature, but a gymnast could also be fun. Or perhaps you have other ideas? If you design your own figure, make sure the arms are freakishly long so the body can pass between the arms when it's swinging.

The cardboard crosspiece serves as a fulcrum.

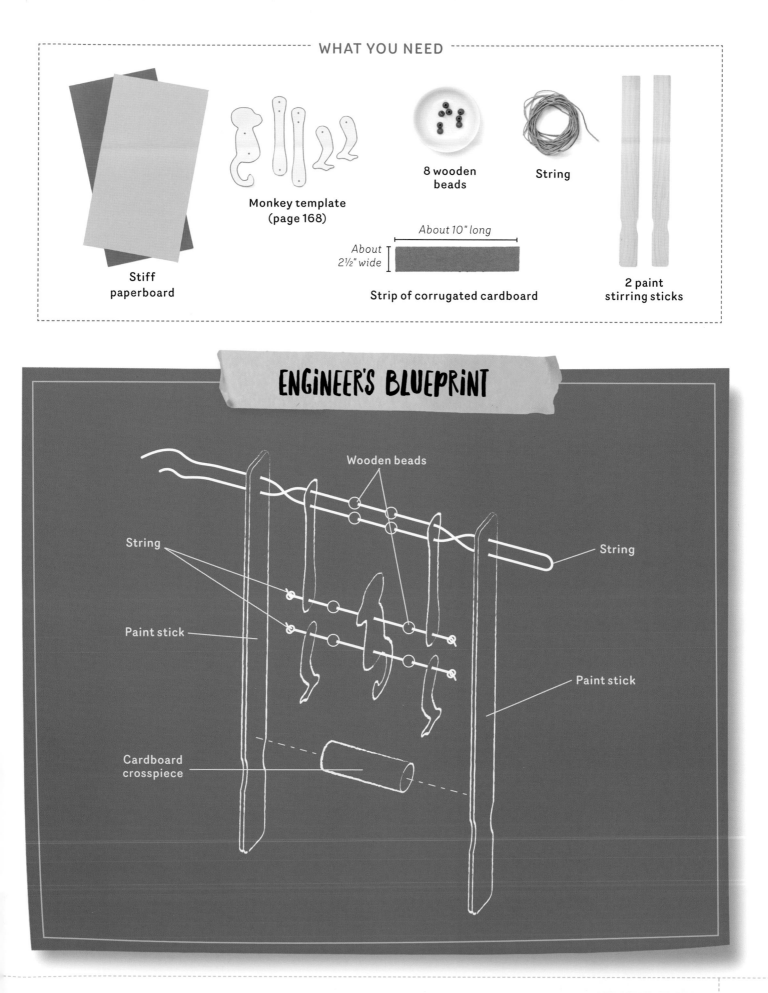

Stiff
paperboard

Monkey template
(page 168)

8 wooden
beads

String

2 paint
stirring sticks

About 10" long

About
2½" wide

Strip of corrugated cardboard

ENGINEER'S BLUEPRINT

Wooden beads

String

String

Paint stick

Paint stick

Cardboard
crosspiece

MAKE YOUR MONKEY

If you have a needle that's large enough to thread with your string, you can use it to "sew" the monkey's body together in step 2.

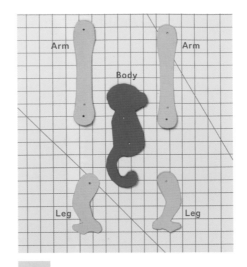

1 Using the Template Transfer technique (page 17), trace and cut out the monkey's body, arms, and legs from paperboard. (Small scissors, like cuticle scissors, work well.) Using a pushpin, make holes in the legs, arms, and body, following the template.

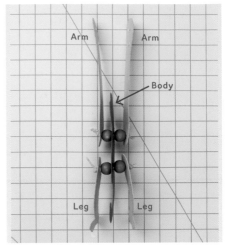

2 Using short lengths of string, attach the arms and legs to the monkey's shoulders and hips, separated by wooden beads, as shown. Knot the ends of the strings to hold all the limbs in place. Be sure not to tie the strings too tightly; the parts need to be able to move.

SPEAK LiKE AN ENGiNEER

A lever is known as a *simple machine* — a tool that makes forces stronger and helps us work more easily (other simple machines are pulleys, screws, and wheels). Engineers use the term *effort* to describe the force you apply to a lever, and *load* or *resistance* to describe the force that results.

Levers fall into three classes depending on the location of the fulcrum, load, and effort: class 1 (fulcrum in the middle, load on the end, like a seesaw), class 2 (fulcrum on one end, load in the middle, like a wheelbarrow), or class 3 (fulcrum on one end, effort in the middle, like a pair of tweezers).

How powerful are levers? "Give me a place to stand on," said the ancient Greek engineer Archimedes, "and I will move the Earth."

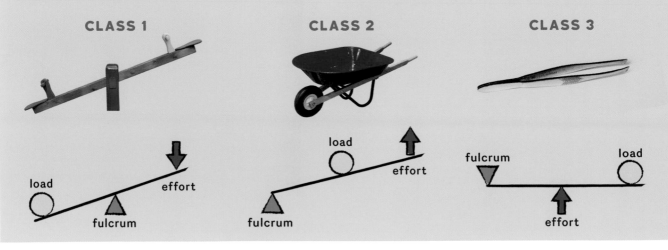

SET UP THE MONKEY BARS

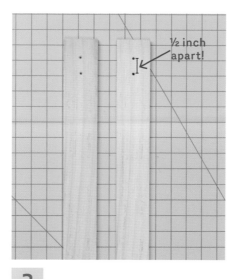

½ inch apart!

3 With a pushpin, poke matching pairs of holes near the top of each paint stick, about ½ inch apart. Twist the pushpin in the holes to make them large enough for your string. (For thick string, you might need to use a small nail to widen the holes.)

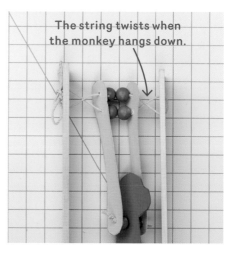

One-third the length of the paint sticks

4 Using the Roll a Bearing technique (page 18), roll and hot-glue the cardboard strip into a tight cylinder. Hot-glue the cylinder in place as a crosspiece between the paint sticks, about one-third of the way up from the end.

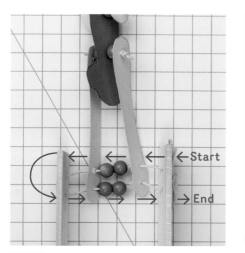

← Start

→ End

5 Set the paint sticks on a table. Place the monkey upside down between the sticks, with beads between its hands. Thread a length of string through the paint sticks, hands, and beads, as shown.

Tie the ends in a bow.

6 Tie the ends in a temporary bow, but don't tie it too tightly. You want some slack.

The string twists when the monkey hangs down.

TEST AND TINKER

Test the swinging action: Holding the paint sticks upright, gently squeeze the bottom of the handles, release your grip as the monkey swings around, and then squeeze again. The monkey should swing around and then back again. Tinker with the string tension, if needed. When the monkey swings to your liking, undo the bow and knot the ends of the string.

CHAPTER 3

SIGHTS AND SOUNDS

AUDIO & OPTICAL ENGINEERING

Everything we see and hear is made up of light or sound. As light and sound both move through space, they obey the laws of physics. Audio and optical engineers use these natural rules to design devices or systems that help us see and hear things in new or better ways. An audio engineer in the music industry might design microphones and amplifiers to help musicians create a particular type of sound. An optical engineer might help develop a specialized lens for a new telescope or a fiber-optic communications system that transmits information using light.

The following projects let you play around with sound and light yourself. With help from the laws of physics, you'll be able to turn a phone into a loudspeaker, see around corners, and create wild visual patterns.

CUP AMPLIFIER

Slide a mobile phone into this low-tech amplifier and the result will be music to your ears. The audio is deeper, richer, and louder, thanks to the science of sound waves and the natural amplification created by the cone-shaped cups.

If the two cups look a bit like the attentive ears of a cat or fox, that's no coincidence. Animal ears use the same science, but in reverse: they help creatures hear by gathering sound waves and directing them into the ear. For engineers, that's a design worth copying. (Biomimicry again! See page 26.)

Customize your amplifier to fit any size phone!

Tabs cut all around the hole make it easy to glue the cardboard tube in place.

Cut a slot with a flap to support your phone.

WHAT'S GOING ON

The Cup Amplifier focuses and projects sound waves, the same way that a cheerleader's megaphone (or even just your cupped hands) amplifies your voice. Once sound waves are created, they want to spread out in all directions. The amplifier directs them from your phone's speakers into the cardboard cups, where, instead of scattering, they are gathered and channeled in one direction — out the openings.

ENGINEER SPOTLIGHT: THOMAS EDISON

Thomas Edison (1847–1931), perhaps America's greatest self-taught engineer, patented more than a thousand inventions over his lifetime, many of which involved light or sound: the incandescent light bulb, the phonograph, and the motion picture camera, to name just a few. Working in his Menlo Park, New Jersey, research laboratory (itself the first lab of its kind), he soon became a celebrity, "the wizard of Menlo Park." While many of his inventions changed the way we live, not all caught on.

One that flopped was his "megaphone," made from 6-foot-long paper funnels (much like our Cup Amplifier, page 45) attached to listening tubes. Edison designed the device to help people who were hard of hearing, and while it did allow you to hear a whisper from a thousand feet away, it was just too big to be practical. Later in his life he said he was working on another kind of listening device, a ghost phone for communicating with the spirit world (he might have been joking). Good thing he had other ideas, like starting General Electric, still one of the biggest companies in the United States!

Thomas Edison in 1878 with an early version of his phonograph

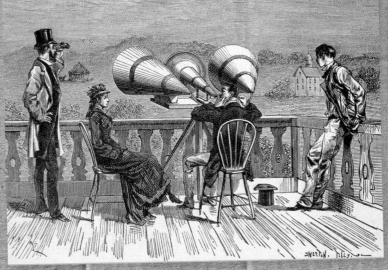

His less successful megaphone

BOX PERISCOPE

Almost since the moment it was invented in the late 1800s, the periscope has been a tool for sneakiness. If you were the captain of a submarine, you could keep your boat submerged and still peer across the ocean's surface. If you were a soldier stationed in a trench during World War I, you could check out the battlefield without showing your face. And if you were a kid with dreams of being a private detective, you could spy on your neighbors from behind a fence. All you need to make your own periscope are two mirrors, set at the proper angle, and some kind of holder. Cardboard for the win!

. . . and your view will be from up here!

Take a peek down here . . .

WHAT YOU NEED

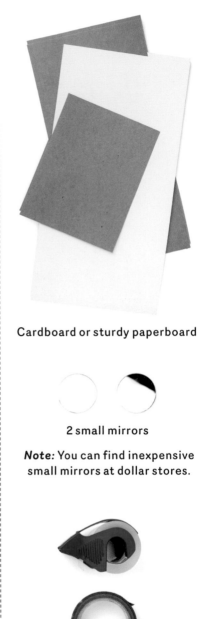

Cardboard or sturdy paperboard

2 small mirrors

Note: You can find inexpensive small mirrors at dollar stores.

Packing tape or duct tape

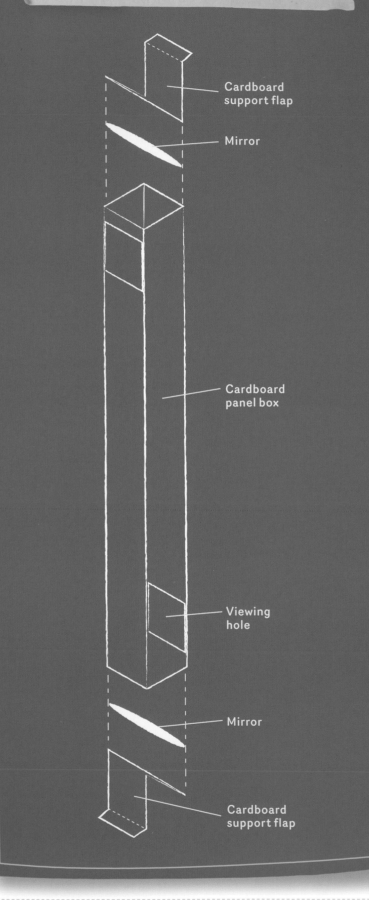

ENGINEER'S BLUEPRINT

Cardboard support flap

Mirror

Cardboard panel box

Viewing hole

Mirror

Cardboard support flap

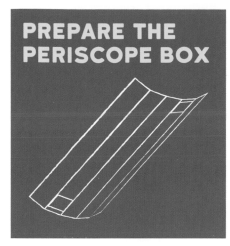

PREPARE THE PERISCOPE BOX

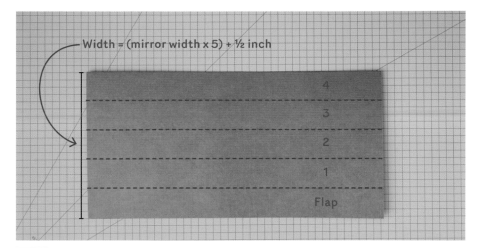

Width = (mirror width x 5) + ½ inch

4

3

2

1

Flap

The height of the cardboard periscope box is your choice, but the longer it is, the smaller the things you see will be. Ours is 20 inches tall.

1 Measure the width of your mirrors. To make a box that will fit your mirrors, you'll need a sheet of cardboard that is five times their width plus ½ inch. (The extra ½ inch allows space for the folds.) Divide the cardboard sheet into five equal panels, marking the lines in pencil. Label the panels, as shown.

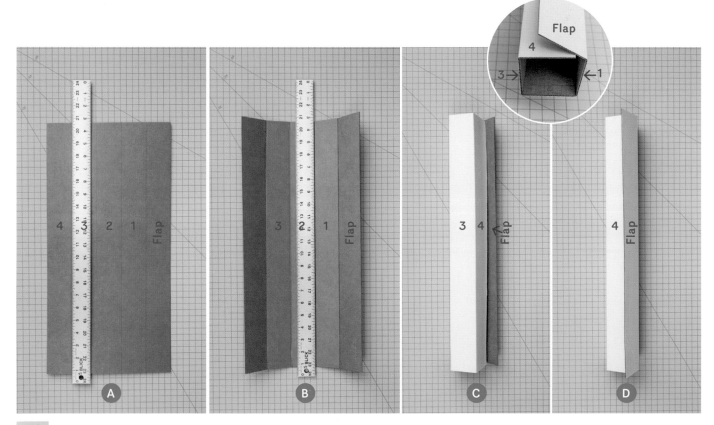

2 Using the Creasing and Folding technique (page 20), crease and fold the cardboard along each of the lines, bending each panel up along a straightedge to keep the fold straight. When you're done, the cardboard should fold up into a square tube.

CUT THE WINDOWS

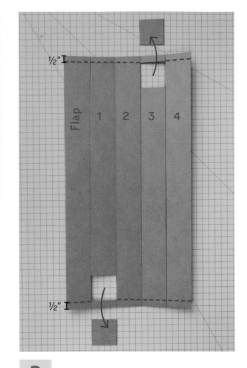

Flap 1 2 3 4

½"

½"

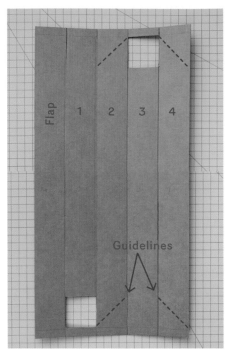

Flap 1 2 3 4

Guidelines

3 Mark and cut a square window at the bottom of panel 1, ½ inch in from the end, as shown. The window should be just a little bigger than your mirror. Repeat to cut a window at the top of panel 3.

4 With a pencil, draw a pair of diagonal lines at the top and bottom of panels 2 and 4, as shown. Each line runs from the top to the bottom of the window. These lines will become guidelines for angling your periscope mirrors.

WHAT'S GOING ON

Light reflects off an angled mirror in a predictable way, sort of like a ball bouncing off an angled wall. Engineers call this the *law of reflection*. So when you point your periscope's lookout hole at something, the first 45-degree mirror sends a reflection down the length of the box, and the second 45-degree mirror sends it out the other hole to your eye. The first mirror reverses the image and the second reverses it again, so it looks correct. If you use a longer tube, you'll see a smaller image. That's why high-tech periscopes, like those on submarines and tanks, use lenses to magnify what you see.

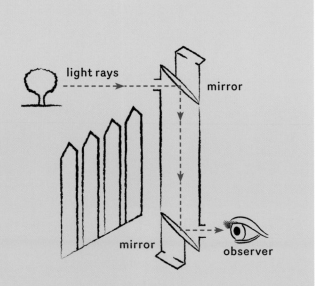

light rays

mirror

mirror

observer

ADD THE MIRRORS

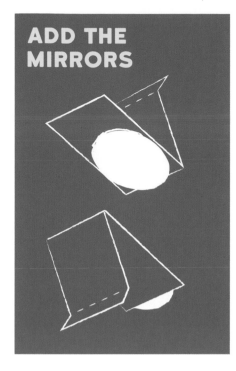

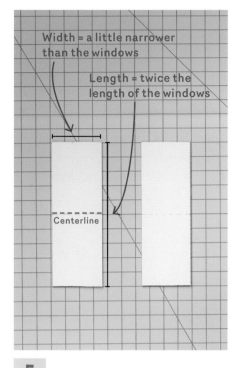

Width = a little narrower than the windows

Length = twice the length of the windows

Centerline

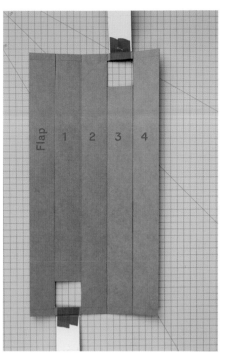

Flap 1 2 3 4

5 From scrap cardboard or paperboard, cut two strips that are a little narrower than the windows in panels 1 and 3 and twice as long. Draw a line across the center of each strip, as shown.

6 Set each strip next to, but not overlapping, one of the windows. Tape the strips in place, as shown.

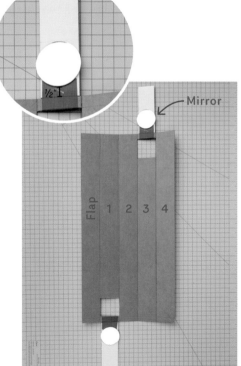

½"

Mirror

Flap 1 2 3 4

½"

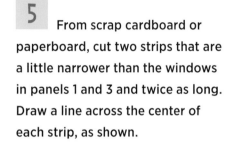

A

Flap 1 2 3 4

B

Flap 1 2 3 4

C

½"

Flap 1 2 3 4

½"

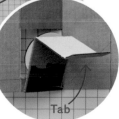

Tab

7 Set a mirror on each strip, ½ inch away from the cardboard sheet. Hot-glue or tape the mirrors in place.

8 Fold the strips over so the mirrors face the windows (A). Then fold each strip in half back toward the end of the cardboard sheet (B). Then fold the last ½ inch of each strip back toward the center of the cardboard to make a tab (C).

FOLD IT UP!

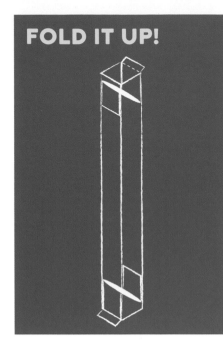

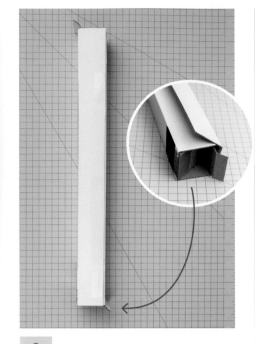

Use the tabs to adjust the mirrors.

9 Fold the cardboard sheet into a square tube, taping the flap to the outside of panel 1 to secure it.

10 Adjust the mirrors so that each one is at about a 45-degree angle, using the angled lines you marked in step 4 as guides. If the strips holding the mirrors are loose in the box, tape them in place.

TEST AND TINKER

Take a peek! Look through the bottom hole and note what you see. Use the tabs to adjust the mirror angles as needed.

Take It Further

If your family uses ziplock bags, parchment paper, or other food wraps, you can fashion a periscope from the long, narrow cartons the rolls come in. Find two cartons that are the same size, open them at their seams, lay them flat, and tape them together end to end to make a long sheet. Follow the instructions beginning at step 3 to cut holes and set the mirrors in place, then fold up the boxes and tape the seams shut.

KALEIDOSCOPE

Back in 1817, Scottish inventor David Brewster called this device a *kaleidoscope*, a name that in Greek means "observer of beautiful forms." Take one look through the eyehole, give the tube a twist, and you'll understand why. Shifting patterns of colorful shapes are produced by carefully arranged mirrors and, in our case, glass beads. Engineering that beauty for yourself requires doing a bit of math — but then the science of optics does the rest.

Get the best view by pointing the kaleidoscope at a bright light.

Rotate the kaleidoscope to see the beautiful shifting patterns of color.

4-6" long

Cardboard tube

Mirrored cardstock (available at craft stores)

Plain cardstock

A piece of translucent plastic

A piece of transparent plastic

Clear packing tape or cellophane tape

Duct tape

Small glass marbles or beads

SPEAK LIKE AN ENGINEER

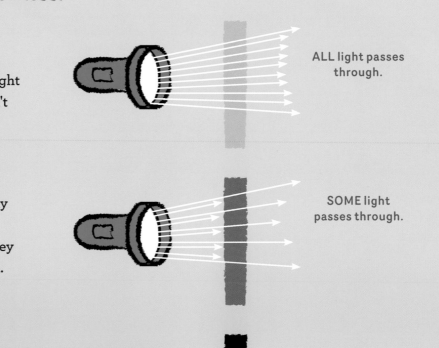

Clear plastic and glass are *transparent*. You can see right through them and they don't block any light.

ALL light passes through.

Waxed paper and the cloudy plastic of milk jugs are *translucent*. That means they let some light pass through.

SOME light passes through.

A material that blocks all light, such as thick cardboard, is *opaque*.

NO light passes through.

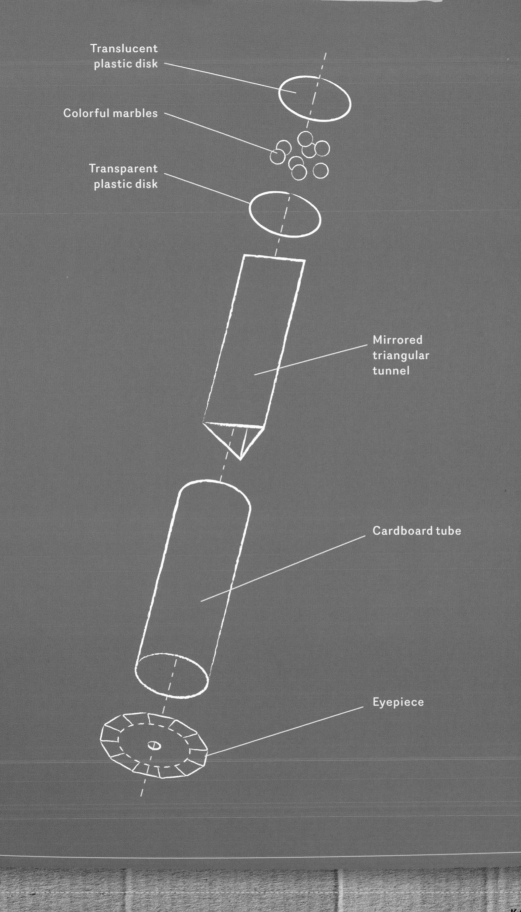

Translucent plastic disk

Colorful marbles

Transparent plastic disk

Mirrored triangular tunnel

Cardboard tube

Eyepiece

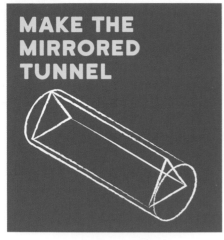

MAKE THE MIRRORED TUNNEL

If you have another reflective material that can be safely trimmed into a mirror tunnel (such as a thin plastic mirror), give it a try. But don't bother with aluminum foil because it doesn't reflect well.

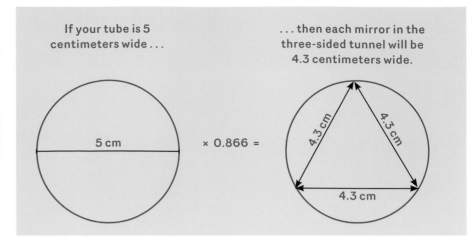

If your tube is 5 centimeters wide . . .

5 cm

× 0.866 =

. . . then each mirror in the three-sided tunnel will be 4.3 centimeters wide.

4.3 cm

4.3 cm

4.3 cm

1 To create a triangular tunnel of mirrors that will fit inside your tube, measure the diameter of your tube in centimeters (cm) and use the following formula to determine how wide each side of the mirror should be:

tube diameter (in centimeters) × 0.866 = mirror width (in centimeters)

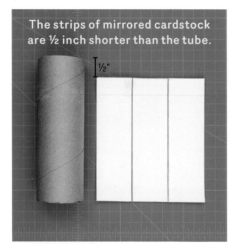

The strips of mirrored cardstock are ½ inch shorter than the tube.

½"

2 Measure and cut three strips of mirrored cardstock, making them the exact width you just calculated. Trim each strip so that it's ½ inch shorter than your tube. Lay the strips next to each other with their reflective side facing down. Tape the seams.

Mirror on the inside

3 Fold the strips into a triangular tunnel, with the mirror on the inside, and tape to secure it.

4 Slide the tunnel into the cardboard tube. It should fit snugly. If it's a little loose, tape it in place, flush against one end of the tube.

*NOTE: At this point, the device is a **teleidoscope**, which is something like a kaleidoscope crossed with a telescope. Look through the tube at something bright and colorful and you'll see patterns formed by the outside scene — similar to the patterns formed by the colorful objects in a kaleidoscope.*

ADD THE MARBLE HOLDER

No small marbles or beads? Other colorful objects can work, but make sure they are translucent so light can pass through them.

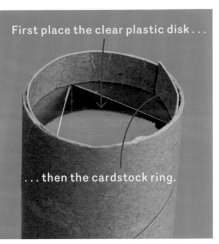

Trace and then cut just *inside* this line.

5 Stand one end of the tube on a piece of clear plastic and trace around it (a marker works best). Then cut out the plastic disk (cuticle scissors work nicely), just inside the traced line, so that this disk is a little smaller than your cardboard tube.

First place the clear plastic disk...

... then the cardstock ring.

6 Set the plastic disk inside the tube, resting it on top of the triangular tunnel. Then cut a ½-inch-wide strip of plain cardstock. Form the strip into a ring and set it inside the tube, on top of the plastic disk, trimming it to fit. Secure the ring with a piece of tape or dot of glue, if needed.

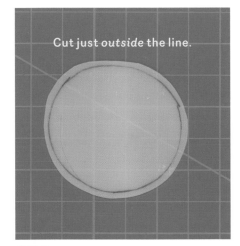

Cut just *outside* the line.

7 Trace the end of the tube on the translucent plastic. Cut out the plastic disk, this time just outside the traced line, so that this disk is a little bigger than your cardboard tube.

8 Fill the ½-inch-deep compartment at the top of the tube with marbles or beads.

9 Set the translucent disk as a cap over the end and tape it in place. (Be sure to use clear or translucent tape.)

ADD THE EYEPIECE

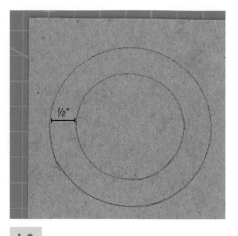

10   Trace the end of the tube on cardstock. Then draw a second, larger, circle about ½ inch outside the first. Cut out the disk around the outside circle.

½"

11   Make a series of small cuts all around the disk, from the outside edge to the inside circle, to make flaps. Cut an eyehole in the center.

12   Place the disk over the open end of the tube. Fold down and tape the flaps.

13   Wrap duct tape around each end to secure everything in place.

GIVE IT A TRY!

To use the kaleidoscope, point the translucent end at a bright light or out a window, look through the hole, and slowly turn the tube in your hand to create patterns. Tinker with the size of the eyehole and how far you hold the kaleidoscope from your eye. Both can change your view of the colorful patterns.

WHAT'S GOING ON

As with the Box Periscope (page 47), what you see in a kaleidoscope is explained by the law of reflection. The kaleidoscope's mirrors are angled toward each other, so the image of the marbles is reflected repeatedly, creating balanced, symmetrical patterns — or, as the device's name suggests, beautiful forms to observe.

CHAPTER 4

BUILT TO MOVE

AERONAUTICS & NAUTICAL ENGINEERING

Aeronautics is the science of designing and building things that fly. For much of human history, however, the idea of creating a flying machine was more a dream than a science. Early inventors tried using flapping wings, kites, and balloons filled with hot air or hydrogen. In 1783, humans began flying in balloons for the first time. Steerable blimps and dirigibles followed, and by 1891 German aviator Otto Lilienthal was making controlled flights in various gliders (until he crashed and died in 1896).

The powered airplanes, helicopters, and spaceships we have today weren't possible until engineers figured out how to build lightweight engines and developed the field of aerodynamics, which explores how objects move in air. Using their new understanding of forces such as lift, thrust, and air resistance, these innovators were able to turn what was once a dangerous fantasy into an everyday event. Similarly, nautical engineers, who design and build boats, study the forces that affect how objects move in water.

To better understand both fields of engineering, try creating your own flying and floating inventions. Staying on dry land is so overrated.

TWISTED PROPELLER

Spin the skewer with your palms and this simple aircraft flies upward. Its rotating blades provide lift, while the skewer provides stability. Be generous with the hot glue to keep the two connected, and tinker with the corkscrew twist in the propeller — it's the key to the spinner's performance.

TIP: Trace around a coin or the bottom of a glue stick tube to get the same curve on both ends.

CUT YOUR PROP!

Cut a propeller blade with rounded ends from a strip of stiff, glossy paperboard (like from a box of popsicles or crackers).

1"

7"

You can tinker with the size and shape of the propeller. These are the measurements we used.

TO LAUNCH YOUR AIRCRAFT, hold the skewer between your palms and rub quickly in opposite directions to spin it, then let go. The aircraft should fly up and out of your hands. (If it shoots downward, spin it the opposite way.)

Holding each end of the strip in your fingers, twist the paperboard in opposite directions to give the propeller a slight corkscrew shape.

SKEWER IT!

Using the Pushpin Puncture technique (page 22), poke a skewer through the exact center of the propeller, and hot-glue it in place.

WHAT'S GOING ON

The key to transforming a flat piece of paperboard into a propeller is that corkscrew twist. The shape of the spinning blades pushes air downward, which causes the spinner to move upward, following Sir Isaac Newton's third law of motion: for every action, there is an equal and opposite reaction (for more on this, see page 83).

Five hundred years ago, famed engineer and artist Leonardo da Vinci imagined a helicopter powered by an upward-facing screw propeller, much like the one in this project. (He drew diagrams of the device but never built it.)

THREE-WING BOOMERANG

With the right launch technique (and enough space), this simple aircraft will circle right back to you. Like the more familiar two-wing, L-shaped boomerangs, our model relies on spinning wings that provide lift, while its rotation makes it turn. We prefer making it small (about 6 inches across) so we can fly it indoors without breaking things. You can draw your own shape, but the wings need to be equal-sized and balanced, so we've provided a template (see page 169).

Give one edge of each wing a slight bend downward.

Bend down the orange sections for a right-handed throw.

Bend down the red sections for a left-handed throw.

Glue onto sturdy paperboard and then cut it out.

Be sure to apply glue all the way to the edges.

DID YOU KNOW?

The traditional two-wing boomerangs used for hunting are ancient. In fact, they are considered the first engineered flying device. A boomerang discovered in a cave in Poland, made from a mammoth's tusk, dates back 20,000 years, and rock art drawings show Australia's native people using them as far back as 50,000 years ago.

TO FLY YOUR BOOMERANG, hold the tip of one wing in your fingertips, with the template side facing you. Cock your wrist back and then snap it forward — as if you were striking a nail with a hammer — to send the boomerang spinning. It can take a little practice to get it right!

TEST AND TINKER

A number of factors can change how your boomerang flies, so experiment to see what works best. The shape of your boomerang's wing flaps is key, as is your throwing technique. You can also bend the wings up a little at the middle, where they meet, creating what's called a *dihedral* angle. Or you can bend the wings slightly down to give them an *anhedral* angle. Don't bend them too much — just slightly either way. You should still see a big difference.

If you're going to fly it outdoors, try making your boomerang from two layers of paperboard glued together. A little extra weight gives the boomerang a wider range.

DIHEDRAL ANGLE

ANHEDRAL ANGLE

Aeronautical engineers use dihedral angles to design aircraft wings. For more on how wings work, see page 83.

WHAT'S GOING ON

The boomerang's wings create *lift* — upward force — as they spin. It flies in a circle thanks to a phenomenon called *gyroscopic precession*. As the boomerang flies forward, the wings on one side spin against the oncoming air, while the wings on the other spin with the air. That difference creates uneven lift, which tilts the boomerang slightly, eventually causing it to turn.

ROCKET BLASTER

Astronaut Neil Armstrong might have appreciated these tiny rockets — all it takes to launch them is one small step for a man. But, please, no giant leaps for mankind! (You might pop the milk carton.) Because paperboard milk and juice cartons are airtight, that small step is enough to send a burst of air down the cardboard tube and up the straw, launching the rocket. It's a simple design that offers plenty of opportunity to tinker. Experiment with the style and size of the carton, the design of your rockets, and the design of your launch tube holder. But — do we even need to say it? — please don't put your face over the launch pad!

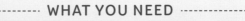

WHAT YOU NEED

Cardboard carton with a spout and cap (like a milk or juice carton)

Paper towel tube

Stiff, glossy paper (like the cover of a magazine)

Straws

Duct tape or packing tape

Cellophane tape

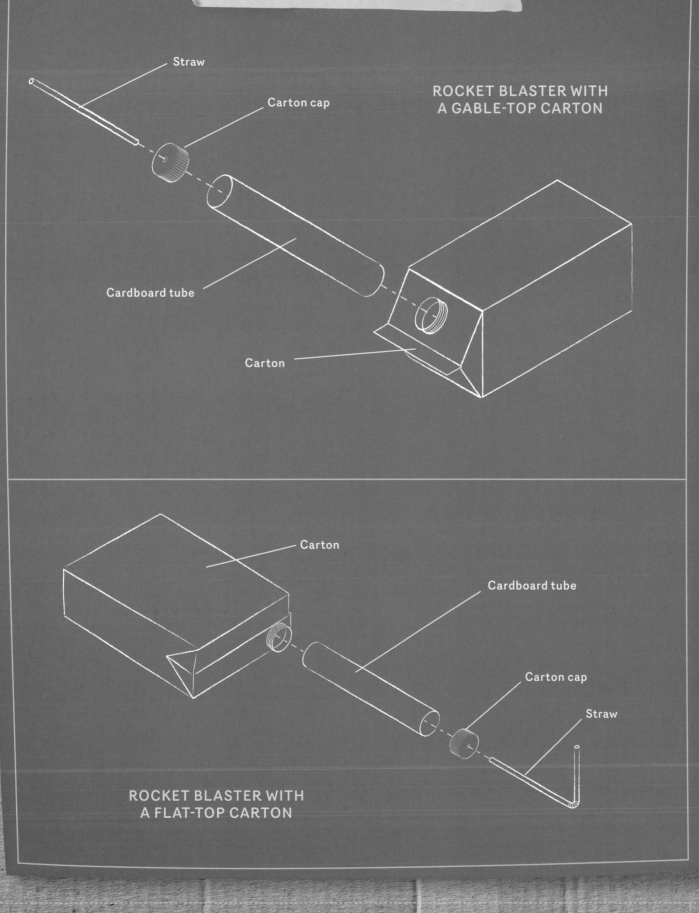

Straw

Carton cap

ROCKET BLASTER WITH
A GABLE-TOP CARTON

Cardboard tube

Carton

Carton

Cardboard tube

Carton cap

Straw

ROCKET BLASTER WITH
A FLAT-TOP CARTON

MAKE THE LAUNCHER

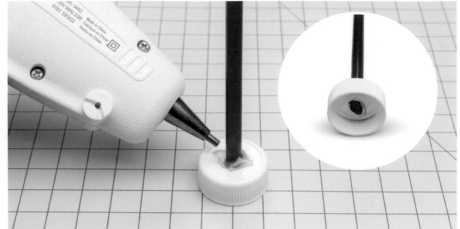

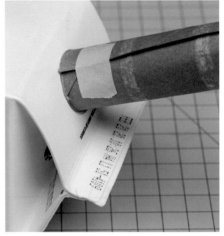

1 Remove the carton's plastic cap. Using the Pushpin Puncture technique (page 22), make a hole large enough for a straw in the center of the cap. Insert the end of a straw into the hole. Run a bead of hot glue around it to create a seal.

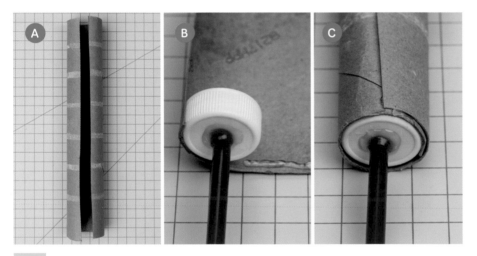

A   **B**   **C**

2 For the launch tube, cut a paper towel tube lengthwise to open it up (A). Run a line of hot glue across the inside edge of one end of the tube. Then set the cap in the glue (B) and roll the tube up around it (C).

3 Slip the open end of the cardboard tube over the carton's spout. Use your hands to tighten the tube over the spout, so that it fits snugly, and then tape it together to secure it.

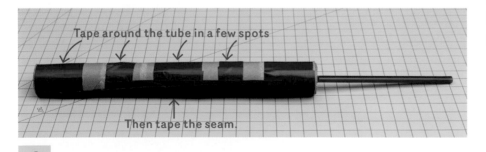

Tape around the tube in a few spots

Then tape the seam.

4 Remove the cardboard tube from the carton. Wrap strips of tape around the tube for reinforcement, then tape the lengthwise seam to make the tube airtight.

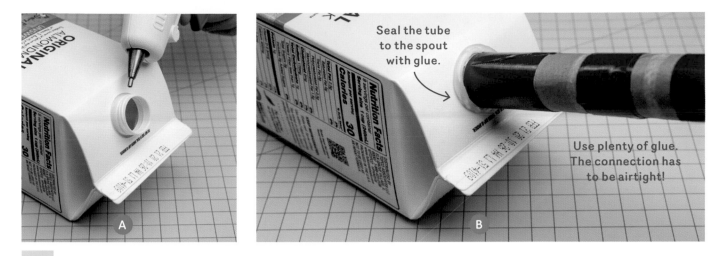

Seal the tube to the spout with glue.

Use plenty of glue. The connection has to be airtight!

A

B

5   Run a bead of hot glue around the outside of the spout (A) and then twist the tube onto the spout's threads. After the glue is dry, run another bead around the outside (B).

LAUNCH TUBE SUPPORT TOWER

For a more predictable flight path, set up a launch tube support tower. We made ours from a cereal box taped to a cardboard base, with a hole through a flap to hold the straw. The support tower helps keep the launch tube stable at liftoff, leading to more reliable flights.

Cut a hole in the top front flap and slip the launcher straw through it.

Open the box flaps and tape them down to hold the box upright.

MAKE THE ROCKETS

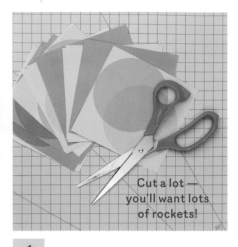

Cut a lot — you'll want lots of rockets!

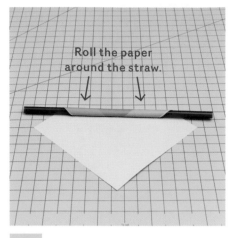

Roll the paper around the straw.

6 Trim stiff, glossy paper into squares roughly as long on each side as the straw on your launcher.

7 Place a straw across one corner of a paper square. Carefully roll the paper around the straw, pressing firmly to shape the paper into a tube, and secure it with tape.

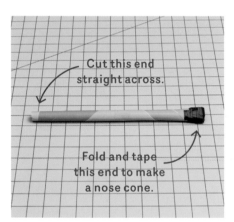

Cut this end straight across.

Fold and tape this end to make a nose cone.

8 Pull out the straw. Snip one end of the paper tube straight across. Fold over the other end of the tube and tape it down. Add extra tape for a nose weight.

9 From more of the stiff, glossy paper, cut three triangular fins. Fold a tab along one side and tape or glue them to the rocket's body, or fuselage. (You may have to trim the tape to fit all three fins on the rocket.)

TO USE THE LAUNCHER, slide a rocket onto the straw so it rests loosely in place, and then either squeeze or step on the carton. The rocket should blast off! To restore the carton's shape for the next launch, blow into the straw.

TEST AND TINKER

If any seals in the launch tube leak, add more glue or tape. And if the carton should burst a seam, try duct tape for a temporary repair.

If your rockets don't fly straight, add more tape to the nose and tinker with the fins. (For a quick test of your design changes, toss the rocket by hand.)

Take It Further

Many cartons can power this launch system, and bigger isn't always better. See what size and brands work best for you. If you use an aseptic container with a spout on its top, use a bendy straw bent upward at a right angle for a vertical launcher. (See the diagram on page 65.)

ROCKET RANGE

Experiment with other shapes for the fins. We found that long fins, short fins, and even circular rings worked well!

MISSILE HELICOPTER

This rubber-band-launched helicopter is a snap to build, but getting it to fly high and spin slowly back to earth may take a little tinkering. That's because, as the name suggests, it's actually two types of aircraft in one. Launched upward by the rubber band, it's a missile that needs to fly fast and straight. On its way down, it twirls like a helicopter, with the spinning blades slowing its fall. Getting it to perform better in one role can make it worse in the other, but with testing and adjustments, you'll be able to strike the right balance. After that, the sky's the limit.

Aim away
from your
face!

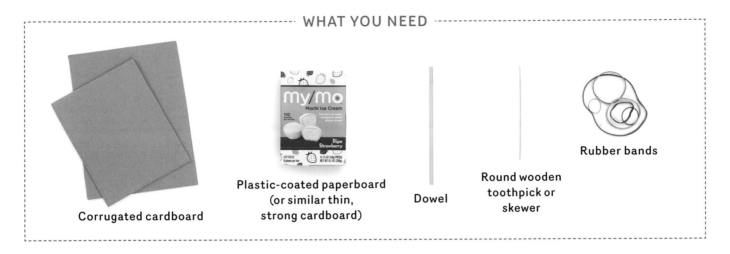

Corrugated cardboard

Plastic-coated paperboard
(or similar thin,
strong cardboard)

Dowel

Round wooden
toothpick or
skewer

Rubber bands

BUILD THE MISSILE

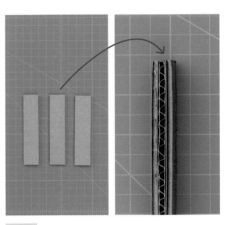

For extra strength, cut two strips with the flutes running the long way and one with them running the short way.

Flutes

1 For the missile body, measure, mark, and cut three strips of corrugated cardboard (ours are about 1 inch by 4½ inches).

2 Stack the strips and hot-glue them together, sandwiching the strip with the short flutes in the middle.

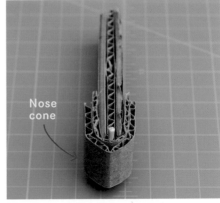

Nose cone

3 Hot-glue a skewer or toothpick to one end of the missile body, as shown. Trim off the points of the toothpick or skewer, leaving two short stubs to make a hook for the rubber band.

4 Cut two smaller strips of cardboard. Fold them over the top of the missile body to form a nose cone, and hot-glue them in place.

ADD THE HELICOPTER WINGS

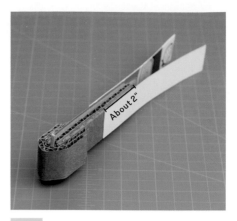

If the paperboard surface is glossy, lightly sand it.

5 Cut two strips from the plastic-coated paperboard. They should be about as wide as the missile body, and a little longer. (Ours are about 1 inch wide and 6 inches tall.)

About 2"

6 Hot-glue the ends of the paperboard strips to opposite sides of the missile body, overlapping the body by 2 inches or so.

Take It Further

The design of the Missile Helicopter is so simple that changing any part of it can make a big difference in how it performs. Try tinkering with:

★ The length and weight of the body — narrow is better, but it has to be strong enough to handle the force of the rubber-band launcher

★ The size and shape of the wings — that diagonal fold is key!

★ The type of nose cone — we tried a cork and an egg carton cup

★ The style of the rubber-band hook — a notch cut in the cardboard also works

★ The type and number of rubber bands on your launcher

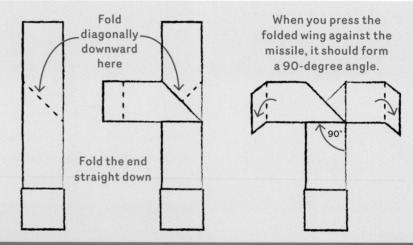

Fold diagonally downward here

Fold the end straight down

When you press the folded wing against the missile, it should form a 90-degree angle.

90°

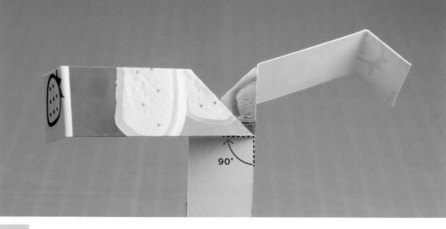

90°

7 At the end of the missile body, fold each wing diagonally to form a 90-degree angle, as shown. Also fold over the top inch of each blade.

MAKE THE LAUNCHER

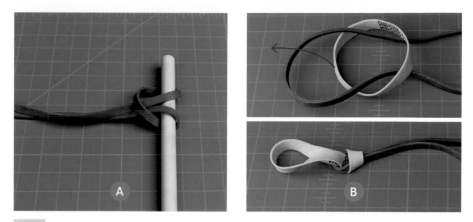

A

B

8 For the launcher, loop a rubber band around the end of a dowel (A), then loop together several more bands to form a chain (B). It should be about as long as your arm when gently stretched.

TEST AND TINKER

Test-launch the missile outside in an area free of trees, nearby roofs, or other overhead hazards. Straighten the two wing blades and grip the ends, place the rubber band on the toothpick hook, pull back the aircraft, and release it so it flies straight up. If it doesn't fly straight or return spinning, adjust the wing folds and try again.

WHAT'S GOING ON

Thanks to their elastic *potential energy* (explained on page 83), the rubber bands power the missile skyward, and the rushing air straightens out the folded wings. Eventually gravity and air resistance cause the missile to stop rising. The nose weight makes the aircraft turn over, the wings spring open, and the diagonal creases cause the blades to spin like a propeller, creating lift and slowing the helicopter's fall. Winged maple seeds twirl and fly the same way. (For more on the forces at work in flight, see page 83.)

Rocket returns

Wings open

Gravity and air resistance slow rocket down

Rocket spins back to earth

Release — wings are flat

Rubber bands provide energy to launch

SOARING SAILPLANE

Few engineering achievements have been as world-changing as the airplane wing — or, more precisely, the wing's curved shape, called an *airfoil*. Combined with lightweight engines, this aerodynamic innovation made air travel possible, which in turn made the planet seem like a much smaller place.

Luckily for us, corrugated cardboard can be curved into an excellent airfoil — but only if you first peel away a layer of linerboard so that it can bend more easily. Then you can glue curved ribs underneath the wings, and the supportive cardboard corrugations will do the rest. Our wing design, technically called a *tip dihedral*, also has angled end sections for stability. (For more on dihedral wing angles, see page 63.) The result is a glider that, with the proper tinkering, can really soar.

The 30-inch wing provides lift.

Tinker with the stabilizer and tail flaps to improve the plane's flight.

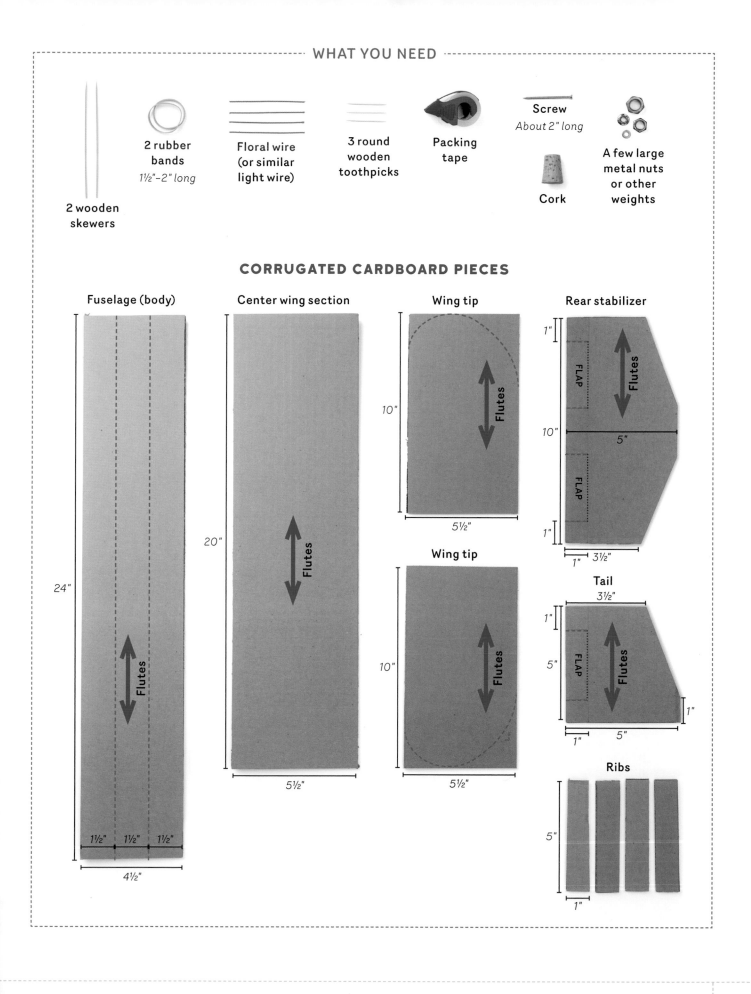

2 wooden
skewers

2 rubber
bands
1½"–2" long

Floral wire
(or similar
light wire)

3 round
wooden
toothpicks

Packing
tape

Screw
About 2" long

Cork

A few large
metal nuts
or other
weights

CORRUGATED CARDBOARD PIECES

Fuselage (body)

Center wing section

Wing tip

Rear stabilizer

24"

Flutes

1½" 1½" 1½"

4½"

20"

Flutes

5½"

10"

Flutes

5½"

Wing tip

10"

Flutes

5½"

1"

FLAP

Flutes

FLAP

1"

10"

5"

1"

3½"

Tail

3½"

1"

FLAP

Flutes

5"

1"

5"

1"

Ribs

5"

1"

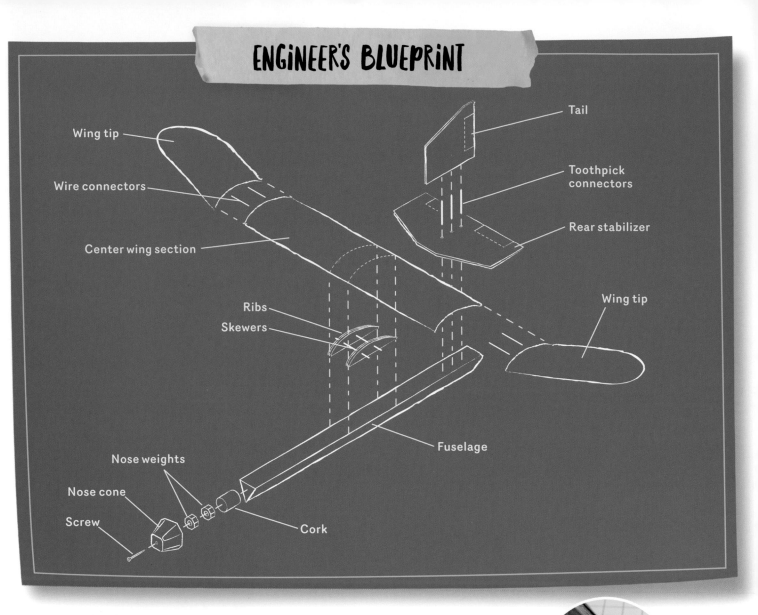

Tail

Toothpick connectors

Rear stabilizer

Wing tip

Wing tip

Wire connectors

Center wing section

Ribs

Skewers

Fuselage

Nose weights

Nose cone

Screw

Cork

MAKE THE FUSELAGE

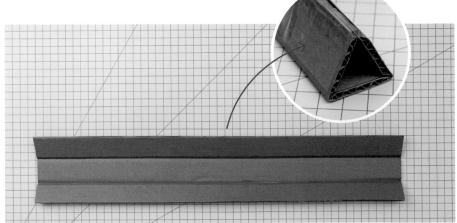

I If you haven't already, use a pencil and straightedge to draw two lines down the length of the fuselage piece, dividing it into three equal sections. Using the Creasing and Folding technique (page 20), crease along the fold lines with a popsicle stick or other tool. Fold the cardboard along the creased lines to create a triangular beam. Seal the seam with packing tape.

PREPARE THE WING PIECES

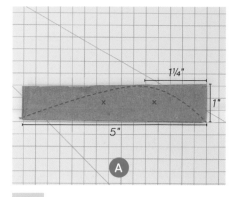

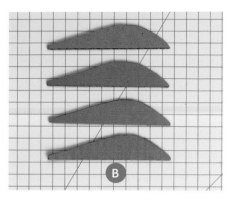

2   Cut out one of the rib pieces, following the diagram above (A). Use that piece as a template to cut three more rib pieces, so that you have four in total.

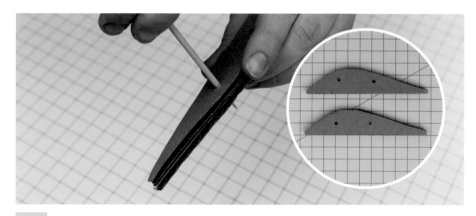

3   Hot-glue two of the rib pieces together. Repeat with the other two rib pieces to create two double-thick ribs. Using the Pushpin Puncture technique (page 22), poke two holes big enough for your skewers in one double-thick rib, as shown above. Use that piece as a template to mark and poke the holes in the other rib.

4   Draw a rounded edge on one of the wing-tip sections (you could trace around a bowl) and then cut it. Use that wing tip as a template to mark and cut a matching rounded edge on the other wing tip.

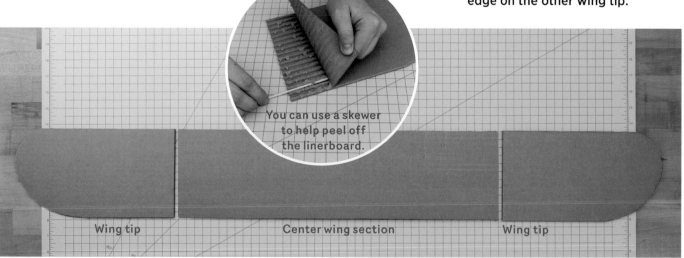

You can use a skewer to help peel off the linerboard.

Wing tip   Center wing section   Wing tip

5   Lay out the wing pieces — the two wing tips and the center section — on your work table. Carefully peel the linerboard from the underside of each piece to expose the flutes.

ASSEMBLE THE WINGS

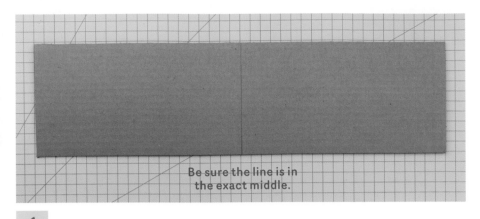

Be sure the line is in the exact middle.

6 Mark a line down the middle of the center wing section, on the unpeeled side.

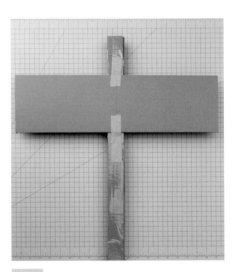

7 Center the fuselage on the centerline, on the underside of the wing. Temporarily tape it in place. (Use masking tape or any other kind of tape that you can pull off easily.)

8 Flip the center wing section over, with the fuselage in place. Mark the edges of the fuselage on the peeled side of the wing. Then remove the tape and set the fuselage aside.

Glue the ribs just outside the lines you just drew to mark the fuselage.

9 Hot-glue the ribs in place just outside the marked lines, bending the wing section to meet the curve of the ribs as you glue. You might need a helper here!

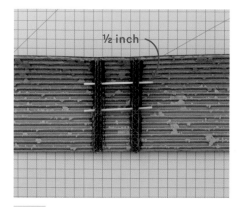

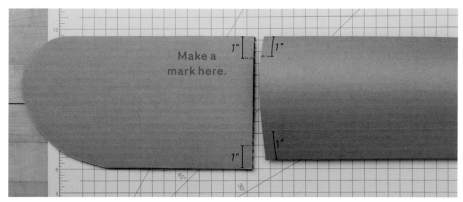

10   Snip two lengths of skewer. The pieces should be long enough to extend beyond the ribs by about ½ inch on either side. Insert the two skewers through the holes in the ribs.

11   To attach each wing tip to the center section, first line up the pieces. Along the edge where they meet, make a mark about 1 inch down from the top and 1 inch up from the bottom.

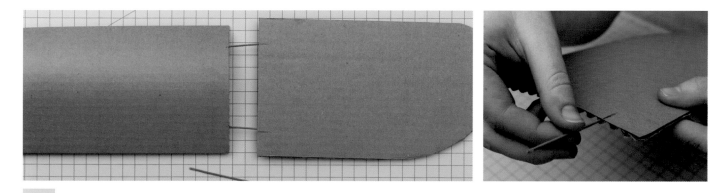

12   At each mark, insert a 4-inch length of floral wire into the flutes of the center section. Slot those wires into the flutes of the tip sections. Tinker to make sure the marks on the wings will line up when two pieces are joined, then dab some hot glue on the wire ends and insert them again, so they are sealed in place.

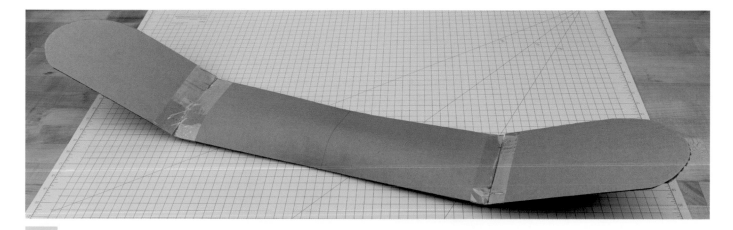

13   Tape the seam between the center section and the wing tips, wrapping it all the way around the wings. Then bend the wing tips up a few inches, as shown.

ATTACH THE TAIL AND STABILIZER

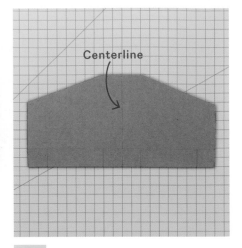

Centerline

14 Measure and mark a line down the center of the stabilizer, as shown.

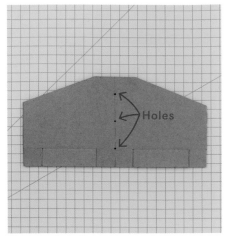

Holes

15 Make three evenly spaced holes, big enough to fit your toothpicks, through the centerline on the stabilizer.

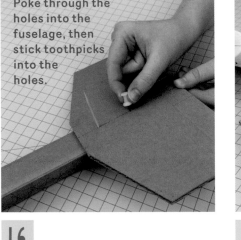

Poke through the holes into the fuselage, then stick toothpicks into the holes.

16 Center the stabilizer at the end of the fuselage, on the untaped side. Using the holes you made as a guide, poke holes through the stabilizer into the fuselage. Insert a toothpick into each hole.

The toothpicks hold things while you glue.

17 Slide the stabilizer a little bit up the toothpicks. Flip the assembly upside down. Apply hot glue to the stabilizer in a line between the toothpicks. Then slide the stabilizer back down onto the fuselage, pressing the two pieces together. Turn the assembly right side up.

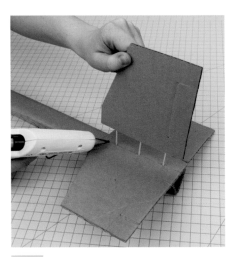

18 Set the tail piece over the toothpicks, as shown. Add a line of hot glue to the centerline on the stabilizer. Then slide the tail piece down onto the stabilizer and press it into place.

FINAL ASSEMBLY

19 Hot-glue the cork into the nose of the plane, squeezing the sides of the fuselage to secure it.

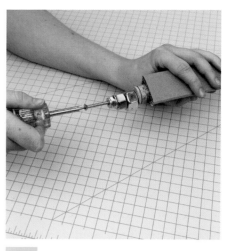

20 Slide two or three large nuts onto a screw. Twist the screw into the cork to make a nose weight.

21 Attach the wings to the fuselage with rubber bands, looping them onto the toothpicks in the ribs.

NOTE: The rubber bands can be crossed or parallel, depending on their length and tightness.

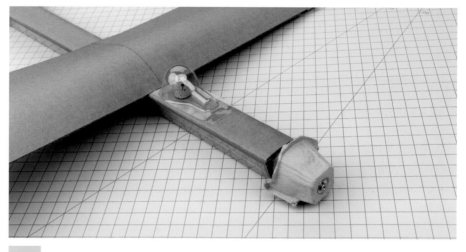

22 If you like, add a cork pilot, a cockpit (ours comes from a light bulb package), and a nose cone (ours is cut from an egg carton).

GET YOUR NOSE WEIGHT RIGHT

The nose weights on a sailplane of this size should total about 2 ounces. We used several large nuts on a screw. If the hole through the nuts is larger than the head of your screw, use a washer to hold the nuts in place. Other nose-weight options to tinker with: a stack of large washers, fishing weights, or even a blob of modeling clay.

TEST AND TINKER

Test the glider's balance: Place a fingertip under each wing, at the top of the curve. Tinker with the location of the wings on the fuselage, sliding them forward or backward, until the plane is balanced. If you have to slide the wing more than halfway down the fuselage, add more weight to the nose instead.

Getting planes to fly is not easy, as all those engineers who tried and failed over the centuries will tell you. So be prepared to tinker some more when you take your plane out for its first test flights.

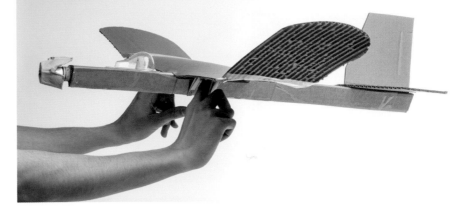

You'll want to fly it in an open grassy area free of obstacles, ideally on a gently sloping hillside. Hold the plane level and give it a firm toss.

If the plane swoops suddenly upward and then stalls and dives, check the balance again, and try bending down the flaps on the rear stabilizer (called the *elevators*), which control the airplane's angle in the air, or *pitch*.

If it nosedives, check the balance and, if needed, bend up the elevators a bit. To correct turning to the left or right, bend the flap on the tail (called the *rudder*).

WHAT'S GOING ON

To understand how an airplane flies, it helps to first understand how an airfoil works. Think of holding your hand out the window of a moving car, fingertips forward, and bending your hand up so the air is deflected downward. Your hand starts to rise. That's Sir Isaac Newton's third law of motion: for every action (air being deflected down), there is an equal and opposite reaction (your hand rising up). This happens with an airplane's wing as well, but the airfoil shape provides added force.

Thanks to something called Bernoulli's principle (named for Swiss mathematician Daniel Bernoulli, 1700–1782), the curved top surface creates lower air pressure above the wing and sends the air downward at greater speed. Together, these effects produce the force called *lift*. The other forces involved in flight are *weight* (the force of gravity pulling down), *thrust* (the force that moves a plane forward, usually produced by an engine), and *drag* (the force that slows a plane's movement, usually caused by air resistance).

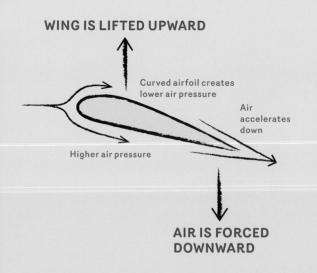

WING IS LIFTED UPWARD

Curved airfoil creates lower air pressure

Air accelerates down

Higher air pressure

AIR IS FORCED DOWNWARD

ENGINEER SPOTLIGHT: SIR GEORGE CAYLEY

You've probably heard of Orville and Wilbur Wright, the Ohio brothers famous for inventing the world's first successful powered airplane, which they flew at Kitty Hawk, North Carolina, in 1903. But a hundred years before that, a British engineer named Sir George Cayley (1773–1857) figured out the science that made the Wright brothers' achievements possible.

Back in 1799, Cayley correctly suggested what an airplane would need — a wing with an airfoil, some kind of light engine (which did not exist at the time), and some kind of steering system. He identified the forces that affect planes: weight, lift, drag, and thrust. He even built the first flying model gliders and in 1853 engineered a glider that carried a person — the first such flight of its kind.

Businessman Sir Richard Branson, founder of Virgin Atlantic airlines, pilots a replica of Cayley's glider in 2003 to mark the 150th anniversary of the 1853 flight.

Many consider Cayley one of the most important engineers in aviation history. And if that wasn't enough, he also invented the tension spoke wheel (which became the bicycle wheel), a self-righting lifeboat, seat belts, signals for railway crossings, and much more!

PADDLE-WHEEL BOAT

As with flying machines, powered watercraft have captured the imaginations of engineers for centuries. And with good reason: without some kind of engine, your choices are either row or wait for a breeze to fill your sails. Some of the first powered boats used steam engines to turn large paddle wheels, a design similar to this rubber-band model. During the 1800s, large coal-burning steamboats were common sights on the world's rivers and lakes. A few are still in use today as tour boats, but paddle wheelers began to disappear after another engineering achievement came along: iron boats with propellers.

A pointed hull streamlines the boat.

The boat's paddles are rubber-band powered!

WHAT YOU NEED

Pint-size plastic-coated paperboard carton, rinsed out, cap screwed on

Quart-size plastic-coated paperboard carton, rinsed out

2 paper clips

Rubber band

2 chopsticks

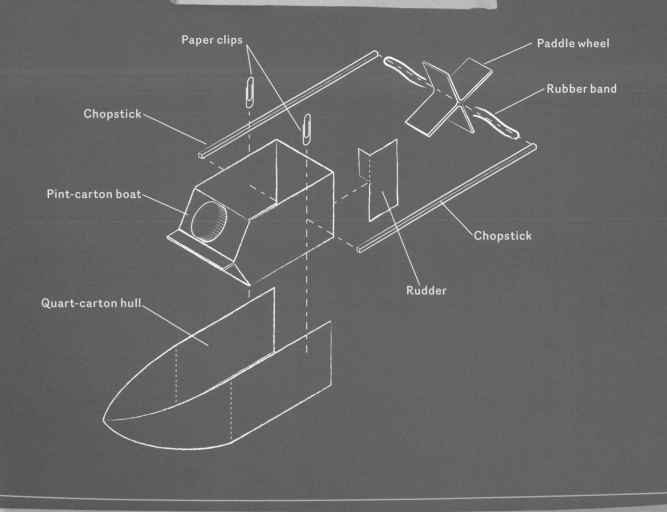

Paper clips

Paddle wheel

Rubber band

Chopstick

Pint-carton boat

Chopstick

Rudder

Quart-carton hull

MAKE THE BOAT

1 Sand the two side panels of the pint carton. (The waterproof coating prevents glue from adhering. Sanding gives it something to grab on to.)

Attach the chopsticks at about the middle of the carton.

2 Hot-glue the chopsticks onto the sides you just sanded, making sure they are parallel to each other and to the sides of the carton.

MAKE THE RUDDER

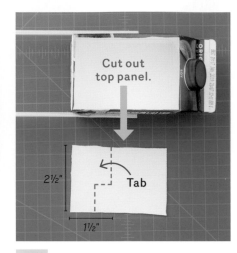

Cut out top panel.

2½"

1½"

Tab

Sand where the pieces will be joined.

3 Cut out the top panel from the pint carton. Then cut a rudder with a tab, as shown, from the cut-out panel.

4 Sand the tab on the rudder. Sand the bottom of the carton. Then fold the tab and hot-glue the rudder in place, as shown.

ENGINEER SPOTLIGHT: JOHN FITCH AND ROBERT FULTON

As with the airplane, the powered boat was the result of many engineers trying many designs over many years. Early steam engines were heavy, not very powerful, and prone to exploding or catching fire — trouble on a wooden boat! The first successful steamboat in the United States was demonstrated in 1787 by engineer John Fitch (1743–1798) on the Delaware River in Philadelphia, and many of the country's founding fathers — in town for the Constitutional Convention — were there to watch. But the inventor most often associated with steamboats is Robert Fulton (1765–1815), who started a successful business ferrying passengers on the Hudson River in the early 1800s. Previously, when living in France, Fulton had engineered what many consider to be the first practical submarine, a hand-powered vessel he called Nautilus.

One of Robert Fulton's steamboats, powered by paddle wheels and a steam engine

MAKE THE PADDLE WHEEL

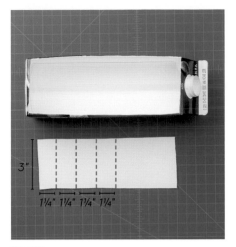

5 Cut the front panel from the quart carton. Then cut four matching rectangular strips from the cut-out panel.

3"

1¼" 1¼" 1¼" 1¼"

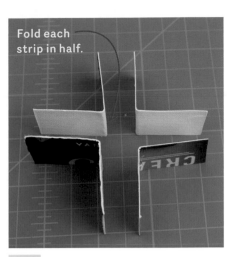

Fold each strip in half.

6 Sand the back of each cardboard strip. Then fold each strip in half.

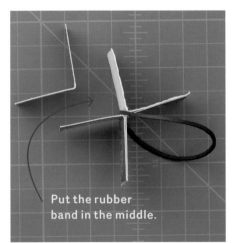

Put the rubber band in the middle.

7 Hot-glue the sanded sides of the strips together to make an X, as shown. Before gluing on the fourth strip, place a strand of the rubber-band loop inside.

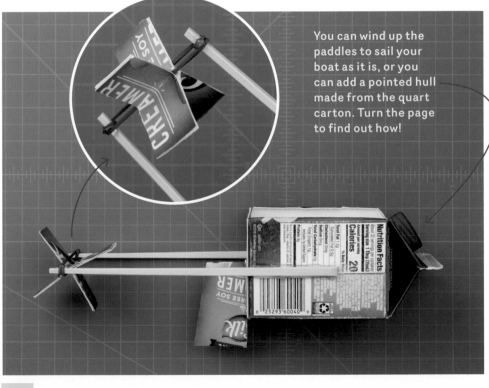

You can wind up the paddles to sail your boat as it is, or you can add a pointed hull made from the quart carton. Turn the page to find out how!

8 Loop the ends of the rubber band around the chopsticks and secure them with a dab of hot glue.

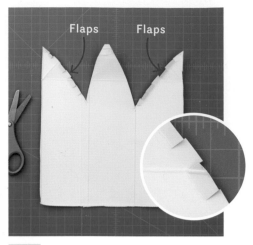

ADD A HULL

Cut along the dotted lines.

Flaps   Flaps

9   Open the quart carton at the top. You already removed the front panel in step 5. Now remove any other pieces of the front panel, including the spout, as well as the bottom panel. Flatten the carton into a sheet. Cut one end of the sheet into three angled points, as shown.

10   Cut a series of flaps into the inside edges of the two side panels. Then fold and sand the flaps.

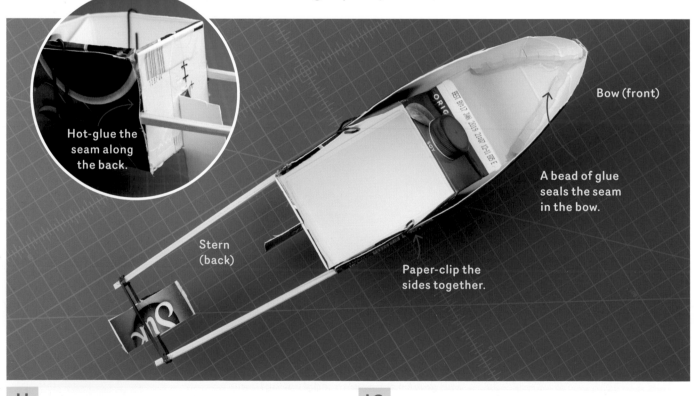

Hot-glue the seam along the back.

Bow (front)

A bead of glue seals the seam in the bow.

Stern (back)

Paper-clip the sides together.

11   Hot-glue the flaps to the bottom panel to make the pointed front of the boat (what sailors call the bow). Run a heavy bead of glue along the seams to seal any holes. Trim the edges as needed.

12   Set the boat inside the hull. Hot-glue to seal the seams at the back (or stern) to make the boat watertight. Secure the boat's sides with hot glue paper clips (or paper fasteners).

CHAPTER 5

ELEGANT DESIGN

MECHANICAL ENGINEERING

Mechanical engineering is all about designing and improving machines — and a machine, to an engineer, is any device that makes doing work easier. Mechanical engineering is thus one of the oldest engineering fields, dating back to ancient times. It was used to build the pyramids in Egypt, the Colosseum in Rome, and the Great Wall of China. Some of the most famous names in science were mechanical engineers: Archimedes, Leonardo da Vinci, Sir Isaac Newton, and Thomas Edison, to name a few. Mechanical engineers use math and physics in their work, so the more we learned in those fields, the more impressive our machines became.

Today, you can thank mechanical engineering for amusement park rides, bicycles, televisions, smart phones, and the many other amazing inventions that make modern life so interesting. The following cardboard projects also make use of physics and math, so they're a good introduction to the field. And like the best-engineered machines, the results will make you appreciate the beauty of design.

FLOATING HUMMINGBIRD

What allows this creature to balance by its beak on the tip of a chopstick flower? A real hummingbird pulls off similar stunts with the help of its remarkable wings, which beat 50 times per second on average (and make the humming sound that gives the bird its name). Our version is engineered from ordinary cardboard, but the secret is still the wings. Pennies attached to the tips keep the bird balanced, offering a lesson in science without making a sound.

We cut the flower and leaves from construction paper.

Weighted wings allow the bird to balance on the point of a toothpick.

For the base, we hot-glued a chopstick to a section of egg carton.

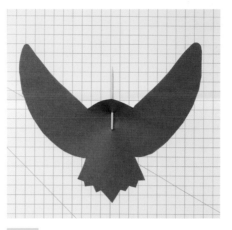

1 Using the Template Transfer technique (page 17) and the template on page 170, cut a hummingbird from thin cardboard, such as a file folder or a cereal box.

2 Use a pushpin to make two holes in the hummingbird at the spots indicated on the template. Then insert a toothpick through the two holes, as shown, bending the hummingbird's head slightly upward.

WHAT'S GOING ON

The pennies on the tips of the long wings shift the bird's *center of mass* — its balancing point — to the tip of its beak, helping to keep the bird steady. It's similar to the way that a tightrope walker balances with the help of a long pole. If your bird isn't balancing, try sliding the toothpick a bit farther in. If the toothpick is loose, secure it with a dab of glue.

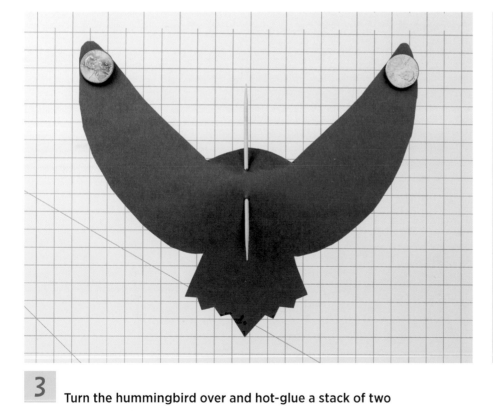

3 Turn the hummingbird over and hot-glue a stack of two pennies to each wing tip.

Take It Further

The shape — a symmetrical U, with two extended arms — is the key to this balancing sculpture, but it doesn't have to be a bird. Anything with this shape will behave similarly. Maybe it's a strongman with two long arms who balances on his chin? Or a rabbit balanced on its nose thanks to its long floppy ears?

ROLLING ROLLER COASTER

A marble rolling down the edge of a paper plate may not seem to have much in common with the latest scream machine rocketing through loops and barrel rolls at an amusement park, but both are being driven by the same physical forces. Gravity pulls both the coaster and the marble downhill, while inertia and friction affect how they move through the various twists and turns and eventually cause them to slow down. This coaster's track is cut from the outer rim of a heavy-duty paper plate. The plate's molded cardboard groove happens to be just the right size to hold a marble — until the forces of physics say otherwise!

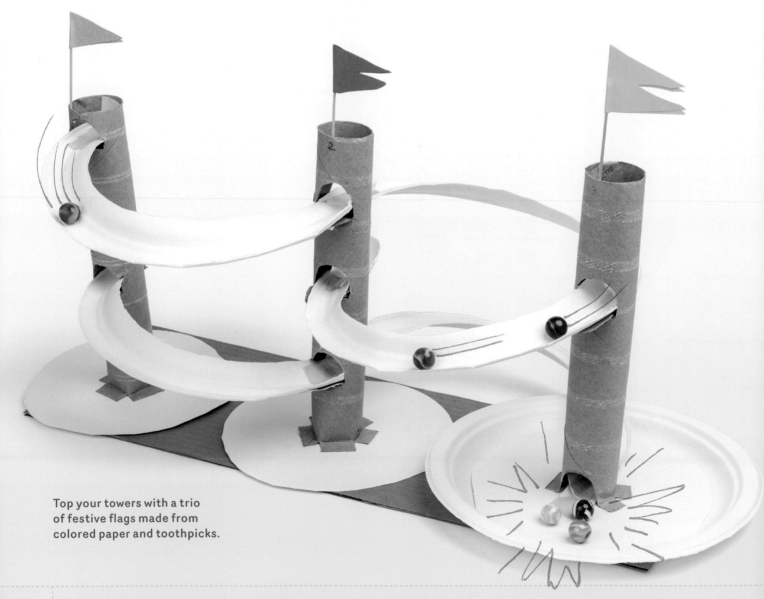

Top your towers with a trio of festive flags made from colored paper and toothpicks.

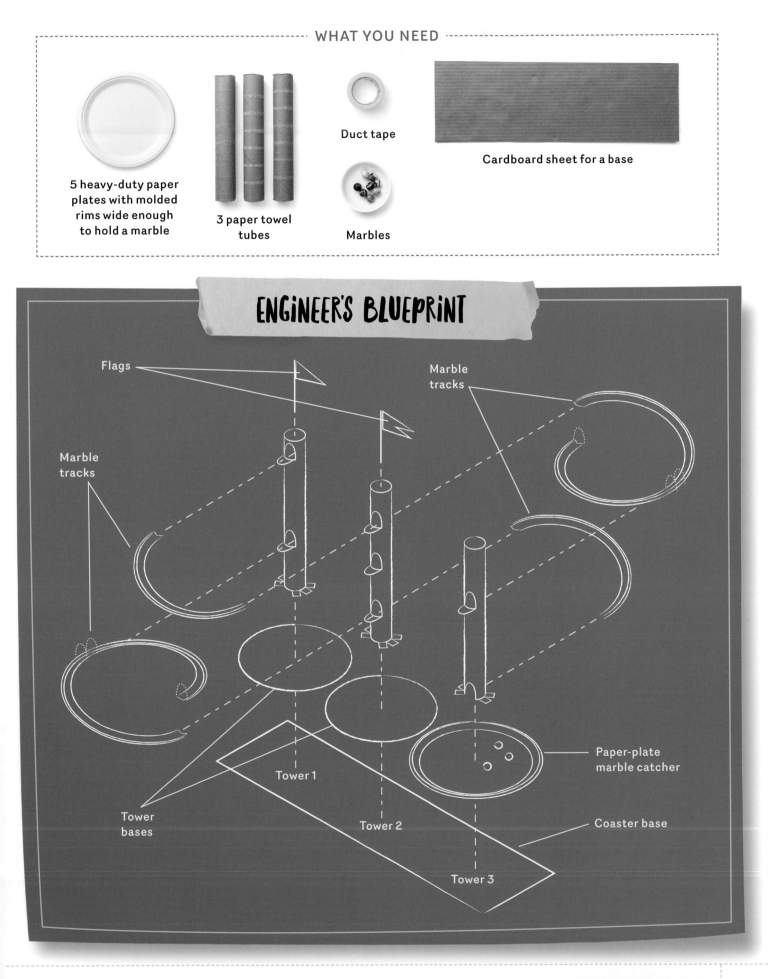

5 heavy-duty paper plates with molded rims wide enough to hold a marble

3 paper towel tubes

Duct tape

Marbles

Cardboard sheet for a base

ENGINEER'S BLUEPRINT

Flags

Marble tracks

Marble tracks

Paper-plate marble catcher

Tower 1

Tower 2

Tower 3

Tower bases

Coaster base

PREPARE THE TOWERS

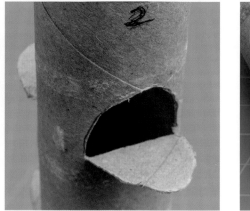

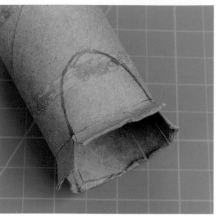

I Use the diagram below to measure, mark, and cut holes in the paper towel tubes, which will become the support towers. Rather than completely cutting away the cardboard at each hole, leave the bottom edge uncut to make a flap that can support the coaster track. Then cut a few ½-inch slits in the bottom of each tube to make tabs for gluing, as shown.

COASTER TOWERS

Cut the upper hole on Tower 1 on just the front side of the tube. All the other holes are "tunnels" that go through both sides of the tubes.

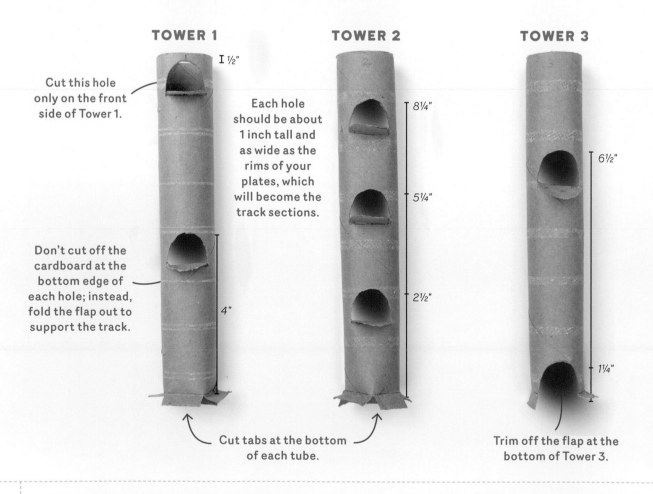

TOWER 1

Cut this hole only on the front side of Tower 1.

I ½"

Don't cut off the cardboard at the bottom edge of each hole; instead, fold the flap out to support the track.

4"

TOWER 2

Each hole should be about 1 inch tall and as wide as the rims of your plates, which will become the track sections.

8¼"

5¼"

2½"

Cut tabs at the bottom of each tube.

TOWER 3

6½"

1¼"

Trim off the flap at the bottom of Tower 3.

PREPARE THE BASE AND TRACKS

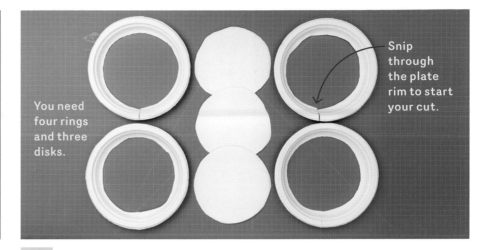

You need four rings and three disks.

Snip through the plate rim to start your cut.

2 Cut the molded rims from four of the plates. These rings will become the coaster tracks, and you can set them aside for now. Three of the inner disks that you cut from the the plates will become bases for the support towers.

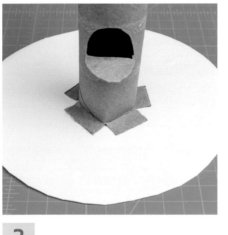

3 Hot-glue each tower to one of the inner disks.

Slightly more than half a circle!

4 Gather the rims that you cut from the paper plates. Trim two so that each is slightly more than half a circle.

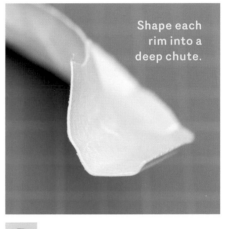

Shape each rim into a deep chute.

5 Bend up the outer edge of each plate rim to form a deeper chute.

DID YOU KNOW?

A roller coaster train or a marble can never roll higher than its starting point, just like a dropped ball can never bounce higher than its release point. That's thanks to the *law of conservation of energy,* which states that the amount of energy in a system must always stay constant. The energy can be transformed into another form (from motion to heat, for example), but for an object to roll or bounce higher than its starting point, new energy would have to come from somewhere — and that's against the law!

6 Following the steps shown below, weave the sections of track through the support towers.

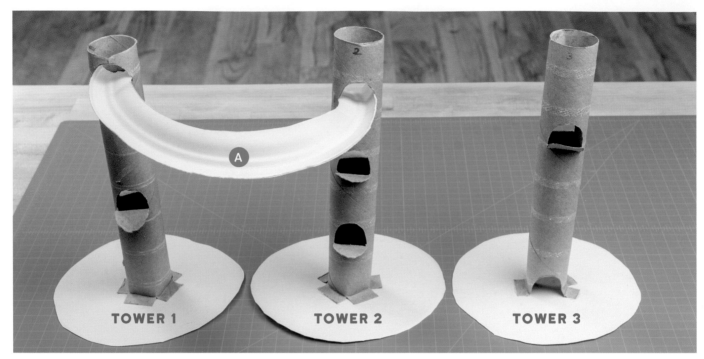

From the top of Tower 1, run a half circle (A) to the top hole of Tower 2.

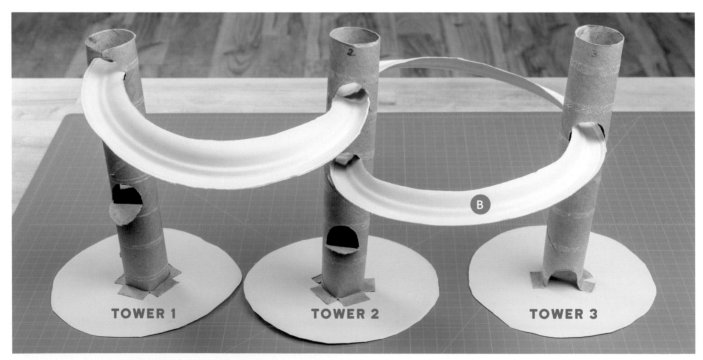

From the top hole of Tower 2, thread a full ring (B) through Tower 3 and insert the end in the middle hole of Tower 2.

Elegant Design: Mechanical Engineering

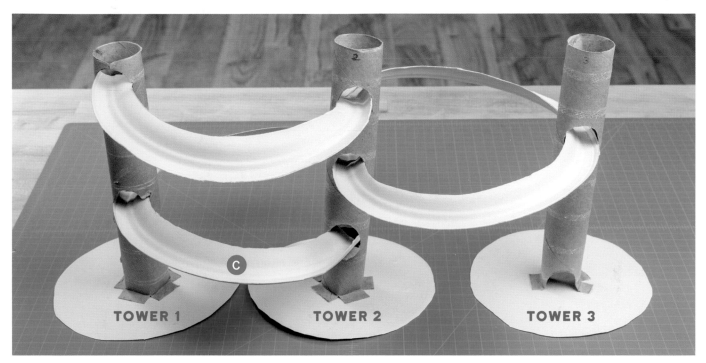

From the middle hole of Tower 2, thread another full ring (C) through the bottom hole of Tower 1 and insert the end in the bottom hole of Tower 2.

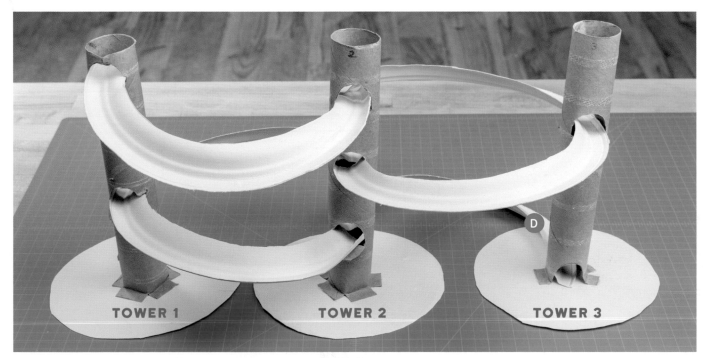

Run a half circle (D) from the bottom hole of Tower 2 and out the bottom hole of Tower 3.

SECURE THE TRACKS

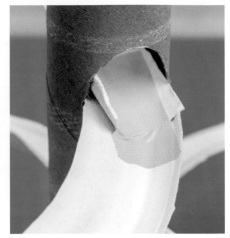

7 Adjust and trim the track sections as needed. Where track sections meet, place the uphill end over the lower end and seal the connection with tape.

8 Test the track with a marble, see where it gets stuck or falls off, and tinker to fix the problem. Once everything is working consistently, secure all the parts with more tape.

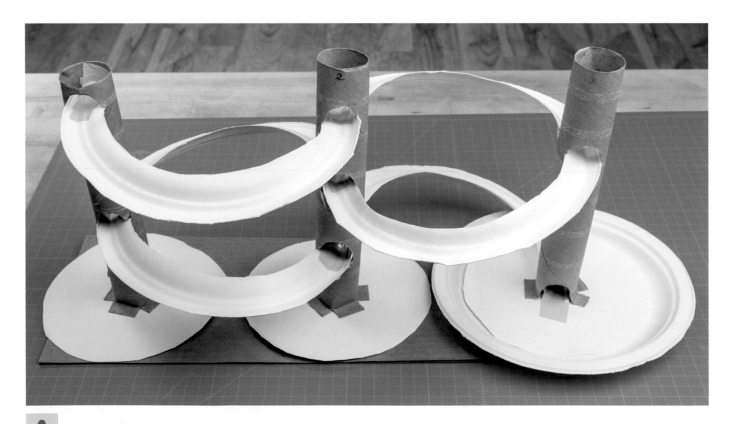

9 Glue the base of Tower 3 onto the last paper plate (to catch the marbles). Glue that plate, along with the bases of Towers 1 and 2, to a sheet of cardboard so that the coaster is easy to pick up and move.

WHAT'S GOING ON

The marbles — like most actual roller coasters — demonstrate the power of *potential energy*, the energy stored in an object. When you lift up a marble and place it at the top of the track (or when a winch lifts a coaster train to the top of a hill), you create *gravitational potential energy*, energy stored in the marble due to its distance from the ground. Once the marble is released, gravity takes over, and that potential energy is transformed into *kinetic energy*, the energy of moving objects. Moving objects, in turn, demonstrate what's called *inertia*, which is the tendency of things in motion to stay in motion until other forces act on them. In the case of our rolling marble, those other forces are known as *friction* (caused by rubbing) and *drag* (caused by air resistance), which steal the marble's kinetic energy and transform it into heat. When all the potential energy has been transformed, the marble (just like a coaster train) stops.

Take It Further

We used paper towel tubes for towers, but long narrow boxes or longer cardboard tubes would also work. And while our figure-eight track packs in lots of twists and turns, you can use plate rims to build any number of other designs (see Chain Reaction, page 146). Add taller towers so you can make your run longer and more twisted. Use other cardboard tubes to make tunnels, or even ramps that send your marbles airborne!

AIR CANNON

Made from an ice cream carton, this rubber-band-powered cannon can shoot a puff of air 20 feet or more. Well, not a puff, actually. An engineer would tell you that it produces something called a *vortex ring* — a fancy way to say an air doughnut. Shooting a gas, such as air, is trickier than shooting liquids or solids, but you can do it inside your house and it usually doesn't upset parents!

Vortex rings do have power, though. Engineers have made large versions of these cannons that can knock over targets hundreds of feet away. They often fill the cannons with smoke to better see the giant flying doughnuts. Search for "air cannon" on YouTube to see some of these in action.

The air doughnut will shoot across the room!

To fire the cannon, pull back the plunger and then let it go.

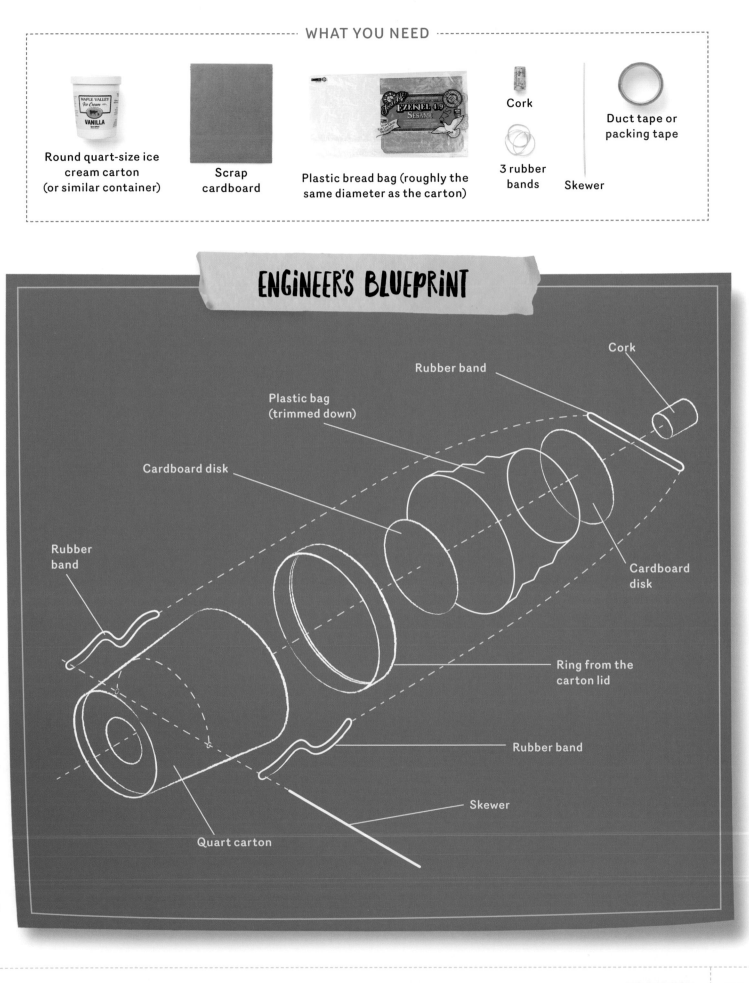

Round quart-size ice cream carton (or similar container)

Scrap cardboard

Plastic bread bag (roughly the same diameter as the carton)

Cork

3 rubber bands

Skewer

Duct tape or packing tape

ENGINEER'S BLUEPRINT

Cork

Rubber band

Plastic bag (trimmed down)

Cardboard disk

Cardboard disk

Rubber band

Ring from the carton lid

Rubber band

Skewer

Quart carton

PREPARE THE PARTS

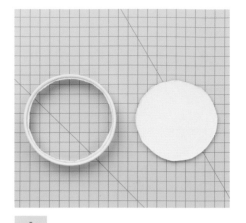

1 Cut out the inner section from the carton's lid. Save the outer ring.

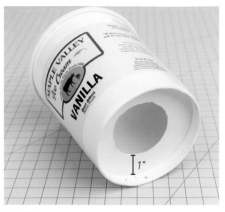

2 Cut a hole in the carton's bottom, leaving an inch all around.

1"

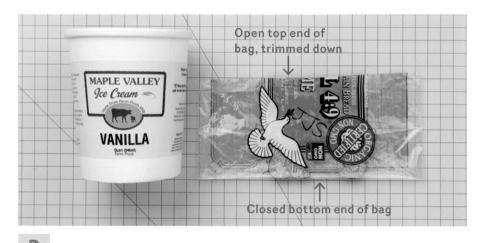

Open top end of bag, trimmed down

Closed bottom end of bag

3 Trim the open end of the bread bag so the bag is about two-thirds the length of the carton.

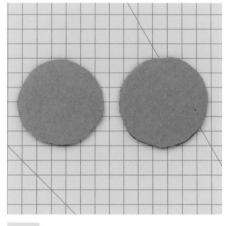

4 Using the Draw a Circle technique (page 19), cut two equal-sized disks from cardboard, both a bit smaller than the carton's bottom.

ENGINEER SPOTLIGHT: STEPHANIE KWOLEK

Creating a gun that shoots air is one thing. Inventing a fabric that stops bullets is quite another. Stephanie Kwolek (1923–2014) did just that. The material, called Kevlar, is used to make the body armor and helmets worn by police and the military, and it's a key component in hundreds of other products that need to be extremely strong and durable. Kwolek was working at the chemical company DuPont in 1965 when she created the fiber that would become Kevlar. She received many awards and honors for her work and was inducted into the National Inventors Hall of Fame in 1994.

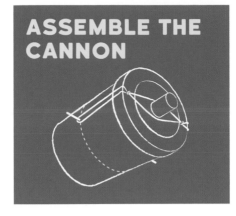

ASSEMBLE THE CANNON

NOTE: Don't touch the plastic bag with the hot tip of the glue gun!

5 Hot-glue a cork to the center of one of the disks.

The cork faces away from the bag.

6 Hot-glue that disk to the outside of the closed bottom end of the bread bag.

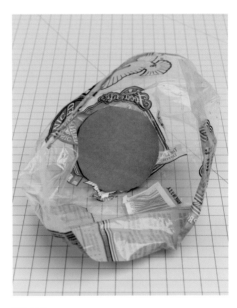

7 Hot-glue the second disk inside the bag, against the first disk, sandwiching the plastic between them.

8 Fold over the bag's open end to form an even edge. Squeeze a line of hot glue around the open top of the ice cream carton and then set the edge of the bag in the glue to attach it.

9 Run a strip of tape around the edge of the entire bag to seal the seam.

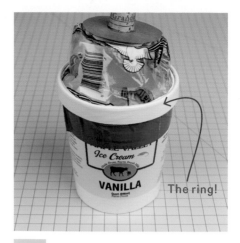

10 Slide the ring from the carton's lid over the plastic bag and press it back into place on the carton.

The ring!

11 Run a final strip of tape around the ring to secure everything in place.

12 Using the Pushpin Puncture technique (page 22), make holes big enough for your skewer on opposite sides of the carton. Push the skewer through the carton until it extends by about an inch out the other side. Hot-glue it in place. Trim the skewer to about two inches on both sides.

13 Link three rubber bands into a chain (see page 73). Loop the two ends of the rubber-band chain around the two ends of the skewer, centering the middle band over the cork.

GIVE IT A TRY

To test how far you can shoot your vortex, set up a candle or a tissue paper flag across the room. Pull back the cork and aim the cannon . . .

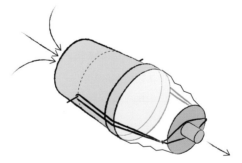

. . . then release the cork to fire!

Take It Further

You can make air cannons from any cylindrical-shaped container: paper cups, oatmeal tubs, plastic buckets, even garbage cans. To see the flying vortex, have an adult help you figure out how to fill your cannon with smoke. Or see if you can shoot a scented air doughnut by adding a squirt of perfume to your cannon.

WHAT'S GOING ON

Like liquids and solids, gases move when forces are applied to them. When you fire this cannon, the rubber bands and plastic bag force the air in the carton out the front hole. The rushing stream of air meets the still air outside the cannon and the friction causes the edges of the air stream to roll back, forming the flying air doughnut that scientists call a *vortex ring*. People who blow smoke rings create the same shape, as do whales when they blow air rings underwater.

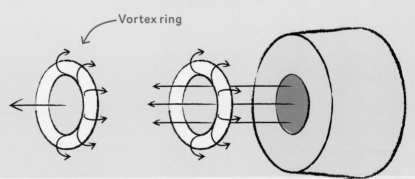

Vortex ring

When the cannon's blast of air meets the surrounding air, it's flying doughnut time!

HANDMADE SPIN ART

You may have made spin art paintings before using a motorized machine that turns the paper at high speed. This cardboard version has some of the same engineering — gears, bearings, a spinning turntable — but instead of being powered by electricity, you crank it by hand (which, come to think of it, is much more artistic!). If art isn't your thing, the gear mechanism can also be used to power other turning devices — perhaps a rotating shelf that shows off your favorite collectible?

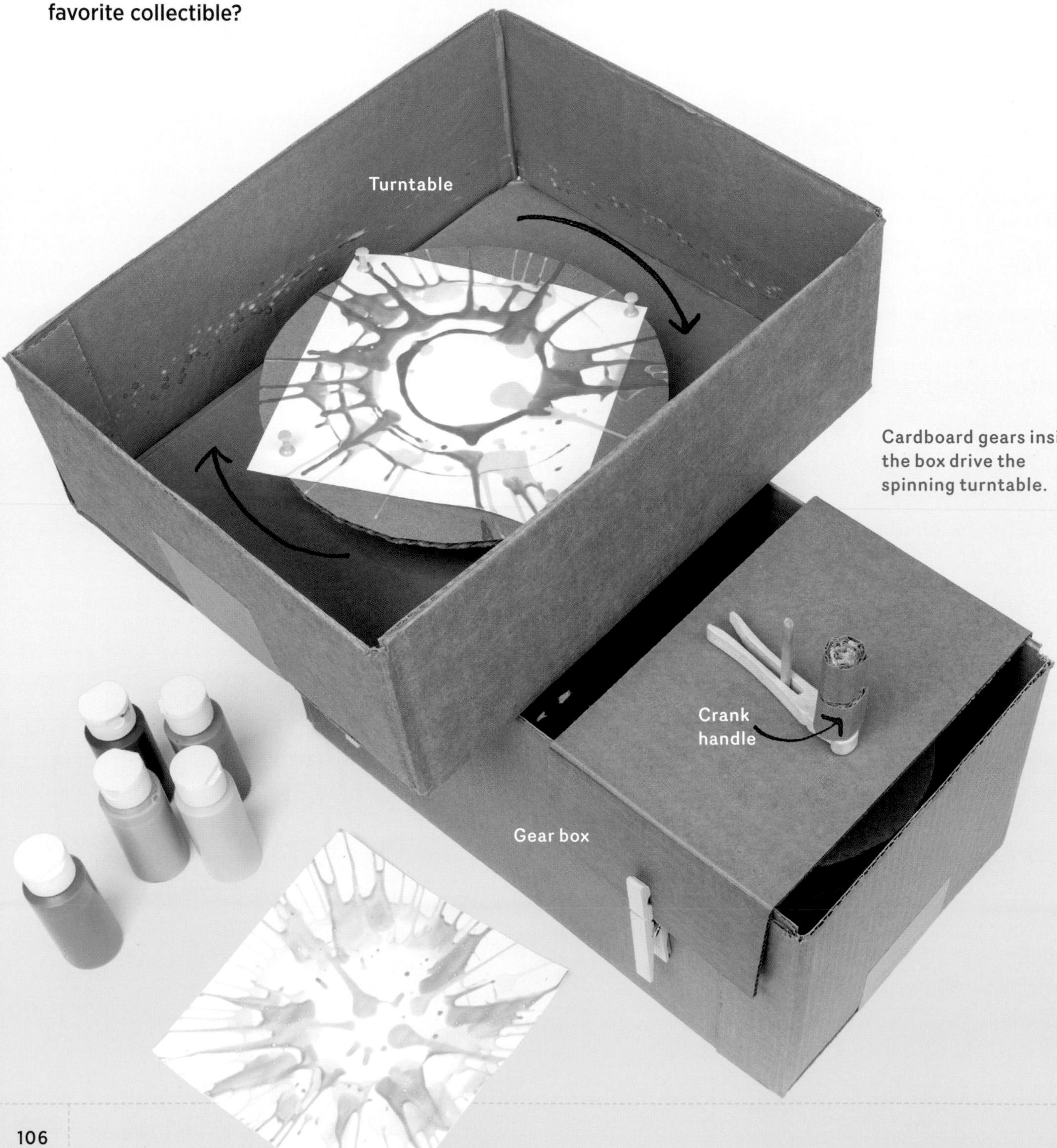

Turntable

Cardboard gears inside the box drive the spinning turntable.

Crank handle

Gear box

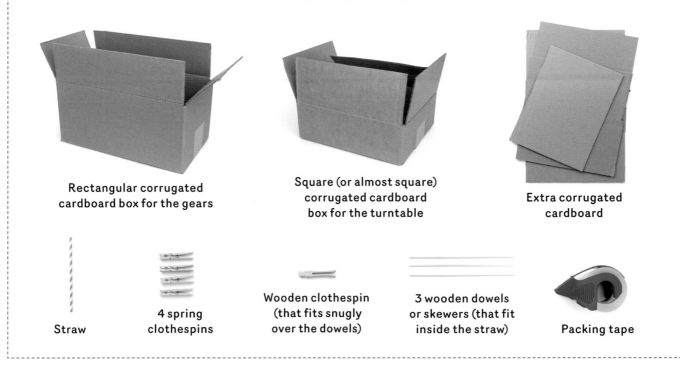

Rectangular corrugated cardboard box for the gears

Square (or almost square) corrugated cardboard box for the turntable

Extra corrugated cardboard

Straw

4 spring clothespins

Wooden clothespin (that fits snugly over the dowels)

3 wooden dowels or skewers (that fit inside the straw)

Packing tape

CHOOSING THE RIGHT SIZE BOXES

The gear box has to be long enough to provide a stable base for the turntable box, with enough space left over to allow the wooden clothespin crank to turn. To help you determine if your boxes will work, set them up as we have here. Lay two clothespins along the long side of your gear box, then set the short side of your turntable box against them. If less than one-third of the turntable box extends past the gear box, you're all set!

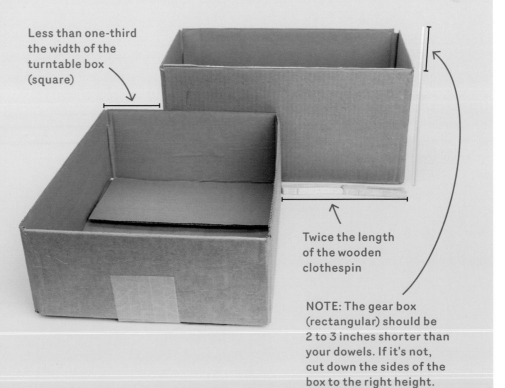

Less than one-third the width of the turntable box (square)

Twice the length of the wooden clothespin

NOTE: The gear box (rectangular) should be 2 to 3 inches shorter than your dowels. If it's not, cut down the sides of the box to the right height.

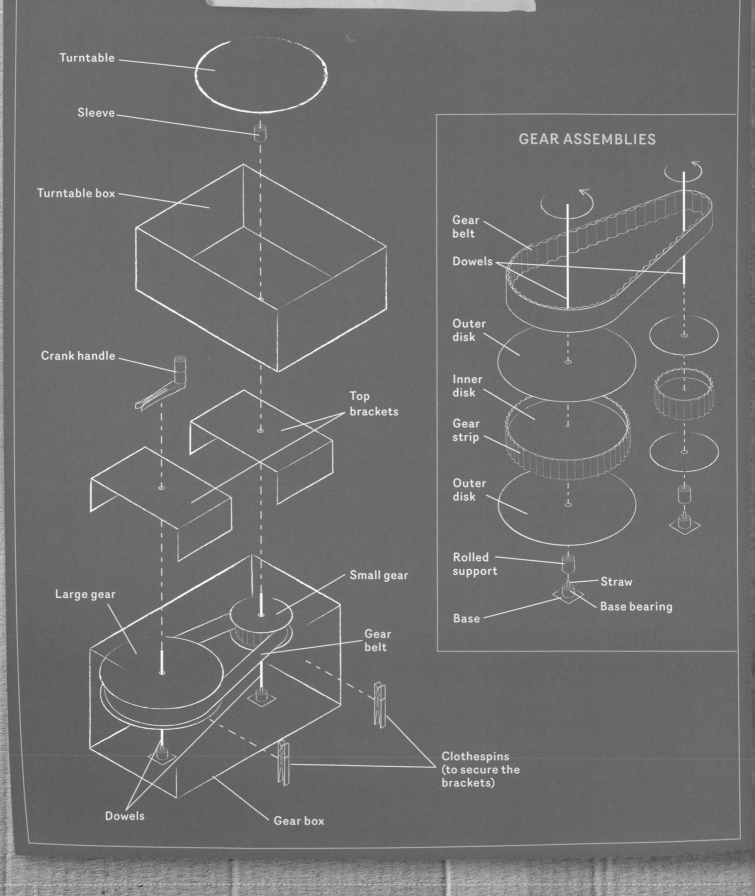

Turntable

Sleeve

Turntable box

Crank handle

Top brackets

Large gear

Small gear

Gear belt

Dowels

Clothespins (to secure the brackets)

Gear box

GEAR ASSEMBLIES

Gear belt

Dowels

Outer disk

Inner disk

Gear strip

Outer disk

Rolled support

Straw

Base

Base bearing

PREPARE THE BOXES

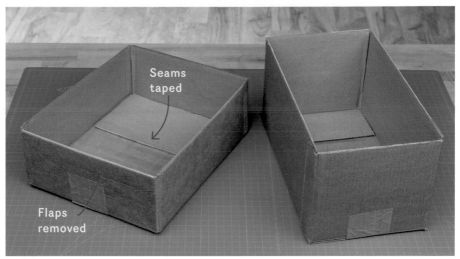

Seams taped

Flaps removed

1 Cut the top flaps from both boxes and save them for later. Secure all the seams on the boxes with tape.

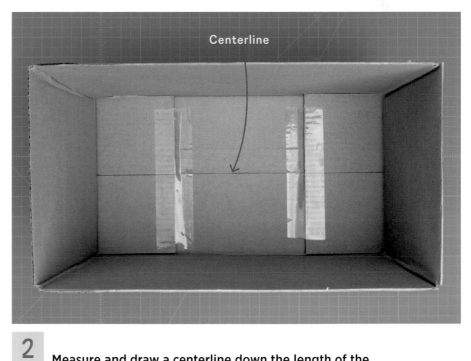

Centerline

2 Measure and draw a centerline down the length of the rectangular gear box.

Gear Assemblies

The spin art machine has two gears, a large one and a small one, similar to a bicycle. Cut the pieces for each gear assembly from scrap cardboard, following the diagram below. These are the measurements we used, but you can tinker with the gear sizes to better suit your boxes. You want them to fit side by side inside the gear box, with room to spare.

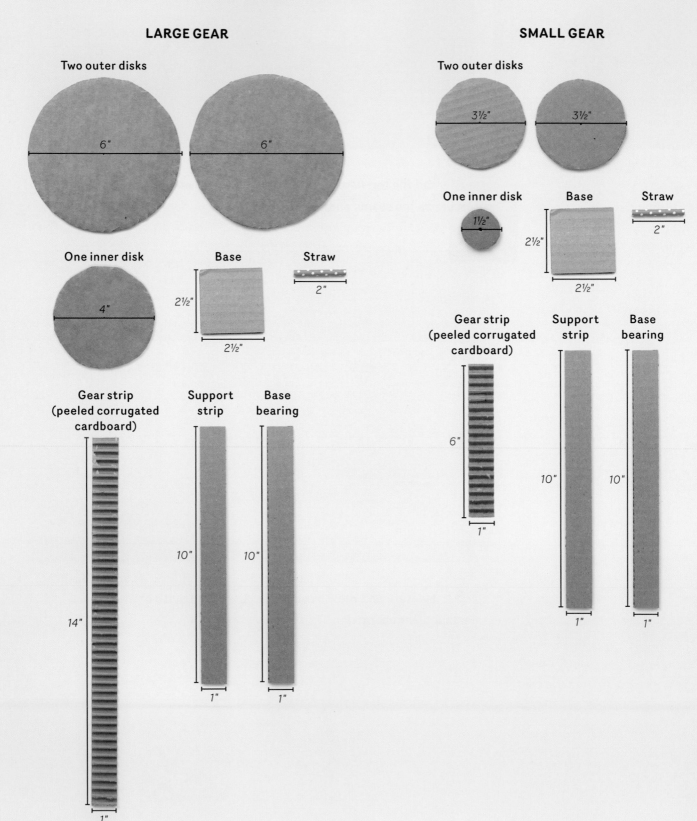

LARGE GEAR

Two outer disks

6"   6"

One inner disk

4"

Base

2½"   2½"

Straw

2"

Gear strip
(peeled corrugated
cardboard)

14"   1"

Support
strip

10"   1"

Base
bearing

10"   1"

SMALL GEAR

Two outer disks

3½"   3½"

One inner disk

1½"

Base

2½"   2½"

Straw

2"

Gear strip
(peeled corrugated
cardboard)

6"   1"

Support
strip

10"   1"

Base
bearing

10"   1"

ASSEMBLE THE GEARS

Center the gear strip on the disk.

3 For each gear, hot-glue the peeled gear strip around the edge of the inner disk. (For a good look at how to glue a gear strip onto a disk, see step 6 on page 134.)

Center

½"

Make sure the pencil marks are aligned.

4 Set the two dowels side by side. Measure the dowels, find their approximate center, and then use a pencil to mark them both about ½ inch down from the center.

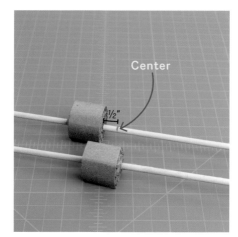

Center

½"

5 Using the Roll a Bearing technique (page 18), wrap and hot-glue a support strip around each dowel, lining up the top edge of the cardboard with the pencil mark you made ½ inch down from the center.

Outer disk

Inner disk

Outer disk

6 Using the Pushpin Puncture technique (page 22), make a hole in the center of each gear disk wide enough for a dowel to fit through it. Thread the disks for each gear onto a dowel — outer, inner, outer — to create a disk sandwich. Hot-glue the bottom outer disk to the rolled support, then hot-glue the inner disk in place, followed by the upper outer disk.

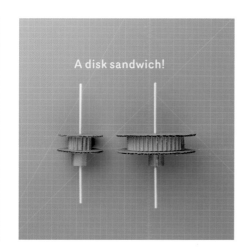

A disk sandwich!

INSTALL THE BASE BEARINGS

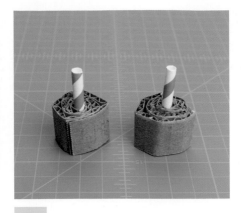

7 Using the Roll a Bearing technique (page 18), make two base bearings from the cardboard strips, gluing them around the 2-inch lengths of straw.

8 Hot-glue each bearing to a small square cardboard base.

9 Place the two base bearings close to each end of the gear box, centered on the line you drew in step 2.

10 Set the gear assemblies in the bearings, sliding the dowels into the straws. Position the base bearings so that the gear disks are close to but not touching the ends of the box. Then remove the gear assemblies and hot-glue the base bearings in place.

The gear disks should be close to but not touching the box.

INSTALL THE GEAR BELT

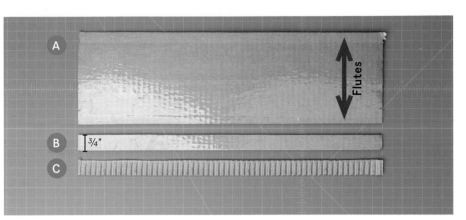

NOTE: Ideally the peeled cardboard that you use in the gears and in the gear belt will come from the same piece of cardboard so the flutes mesh exactly. But the gears will spin even if the flutes are a little different.

11 Set a piece of corrugated cardboard on your work table with the flutes running vertically. Apply several rows of tape to cover the top side of the cardboard (A). Cut the cardboard into ¾-inch-wide strips (B). Then flip the strips over and, using the Peeling Corrugated Cardboard technique (page 21), peel the linerboard from the untaped side of each piece (C). Tape the strips together to form one long piece about twice the length of the gear box.

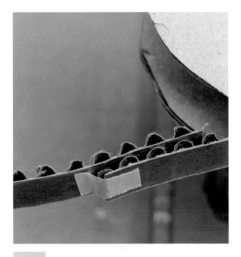

12 Set the two gear assemblies into the base bearings in the gear box. Loop the long gear strip around the two gears, overlapping the ends and securing them with a bit of masking tape. It should wrap closely around the two gears, though not so tightly that it pulls the dowels inward.

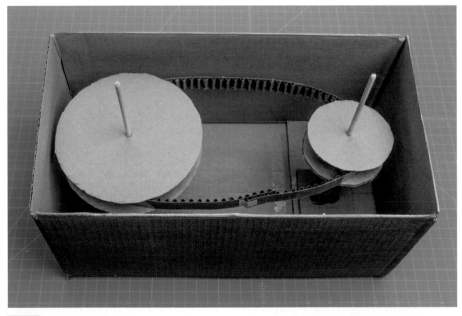

13 Turn the gears by hand. The gear strip should run easily between them, without coming loose or binding up. Adjust the length of the gear strip as needed, repositioning the masking tape. When you're satisfied with it, cut the gear strip to the right length and tape the ends together with packing tape.

MAKE THE TOP BRACKETS

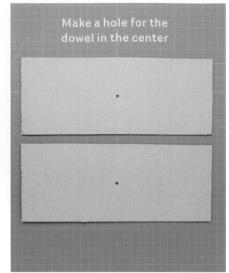

Make a hole for the dowel in the center

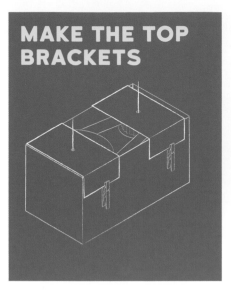

14 Cut two rectangular brackets from scrap cardboard, long enough to hang over the edges of the gear box by a couple of inches. Using the Pushpin Puncture technique (page 22), make a hole for the dowel in the center of each bracket.

15 Set the brackets on top of the gear assemblies, sliding the dowels through the holes. Make sure that the dowels are standing up straight, and then mark where the brackets meet the sides of the box.

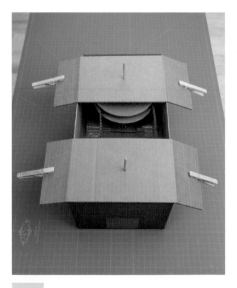

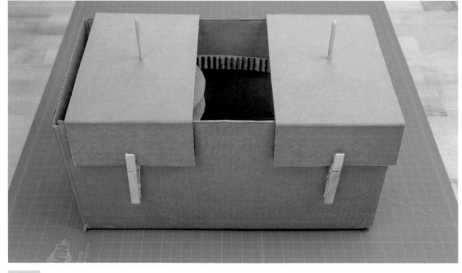

16 Remove the brackets, fold them where you marked them, and then put them back on. Attach a spring clothespin to each side flap, so that it hangs down.

17 Hot-glue the clothespins to the sides of the box.

ATTACH THE TURNTABLE

18 Using the Pushpin Puncture technique (page 22), make a hole for the small gear dowel in the middle of the square turntable box. Set the box over the dowel.

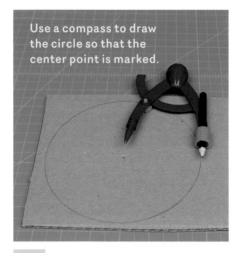

Use a compass to draw the circle so that the center point is marked.

19 Cut a cardboard disk that fits, with room to spare, inside the turntable box.

Don't glue the cardboard to the dowel!

20 Cut a strip of cardboard about 1½ inches wide and 10 inches long. Using the Roll a Bearing technique (page 18), make a sleeve, rolling the cardboard up around the remaining dowel. (But don't glue it to the dowel!)

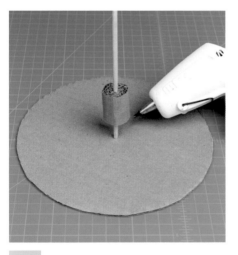

21 Set the dowel (with the rolled sleeve still in place) on the center point of the disk. Apply hot glue around the dowel (but not *on* the dowel), then slide the sleeve down onto the disk and press it into the glue. Pull out the dowel.

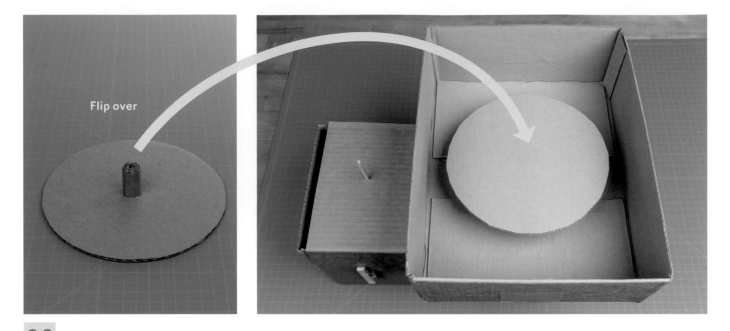

Flip over

22 Flip the turntable disk over and fit it onto the small gear dowel, slipping the dowel into the sleeve glued to the bottom of the disk. If the bearing doesn't fit snugly, remove it and wrap some masking tape around the top of the dowel to make it thicker. You want the turntable to stay firmly in place, but you should still be able to remove it so that you can lift off the turntable box and access the gears.

ENGINEER SPOTLIGHT: ELIJAH McCOY

Elijah McCoy (1844–1929) was a remarkable inventor and engineer who overcame hardship to achieve success. His mother and father were enslaved people who escaped from Kentucky to Canada using the Underground Railroad. Sent to Scotland at age 15 to become an apprentice, Elijah earned his certification as a mechanical engineer and then rejoined his family in Michigan and began working for the railroad.

Before long, he was inventing devices to improve the trains, most notably one that automatically oiled the engines. Over his lifetime he patented more than 50 inventions, including a folding ironing board and a lawn sprinkler. According to some stories, his engine-oiling device was copied by other people, but their designs were inferior, and so railroad workers would request his by name, asking for "the real McCoy" — an expression you still hear today.

MAKE THE CRANK HANDLE

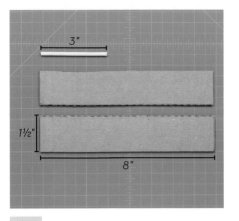

23 Cut a 3-inch length of dowel. Cut two strips of cardboard, each about 1½ inches wide and 8 inches long.

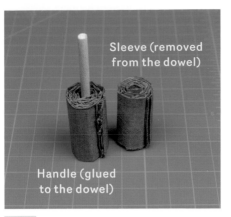

Sleeve (removed from the dowel)

Handle (glued to the dowel)

24 Using the Roll a Bearing technique (page 18), make another sleeve, rolling one of the cardboard strips around the dowel and then sliding it off. Roll up the other strip as a handle, gluing this one around the end of the dowel.

Take It Further

Because gear belts (like bike chains) sometimes come off, we've designed our spin art machine so it can be easily taken apart, with a removable crank handle, turntable, and brackets. If your crank and turntable slip, however, consider gluing them in place. You can still access the gears by removing the brackets, but reassembling the device will require a bit more tinkering.

25 Hot-glue the rolled-up sleeve to the head of the wooden clothespin.

The crank handle turns the large gear.

26 Slide the clothespin onto the dowel of the large gear. Set the rotating handle in place, as shown.

GIVE IT A TRY!

Trim a piece of paper so it fits on the turntable. Thumbtack the corners to the turntable to hold it in place. Turn the crank (or have an assistant help) while you drip tempera paint onto the spinning paper. Experiment with the paint and turntable speed. If the paint doesn't spin outward as much as you'd like, try thinning it with water.

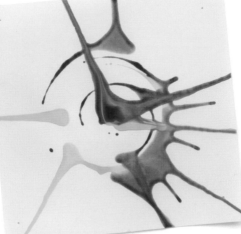

WHAT'S GOING ON

Spin art gets its distinctive look from *centrifugal force*, the spinning energy that drives the wet paint toward the outer edges of the paper the same way that a salad spinner drives water off lettuce or a spinning washing machine wrings out clothes. How fast you crank determines how much force is created, and how much the paint moves. The thickness of the paint — what engineers call its *viscosity* — will also affect how it spreads.

CHAPTER 6

WE'VE GOT THE POWER

HARNESSING ENERGY

Today's energy engineers are developing new ways to tap the power of the sun, wind, and waves, as well as improving how efficiently we use the energy we already have. This is one of the newer fields of engineering, but we humans have been using nature as a source of power for centuries. Windmills, greenhouses, and sailboats were all designed by engineers to capture a force and get something done, whether it was grinding grain, growing plants in winter, or traveling across the seas.

Energy engineers use physics, math, and chemistry in their work as they try to develop sources of energy that are environmentally friendly and sustainable. The following projects let you see how various types of energy can power your own creations. A solar oven lets you bake a cheese sandwich with sunlight, wind drives the wheels of a model tractor, and a rubber band stores and releases energy to send a toy racer rolling across the floor. Feel the power!

BIG WHEEL

You may have seen model airplanes powered by rubber bands. But a car? Not likely. Partly it's because getting wheels to move a car along the ground takes more energy and engineering than getting a model plane's propeller to spin in the air. This design solves that problem by making the car essentially one big wheel and by using a winding stick that makes it easy to twist up the rubber-band power supply. Set the Big Wheel on a smooth floor and it will roll for yards on a single winding. What's at work? It's the concept of elastic potential energy.

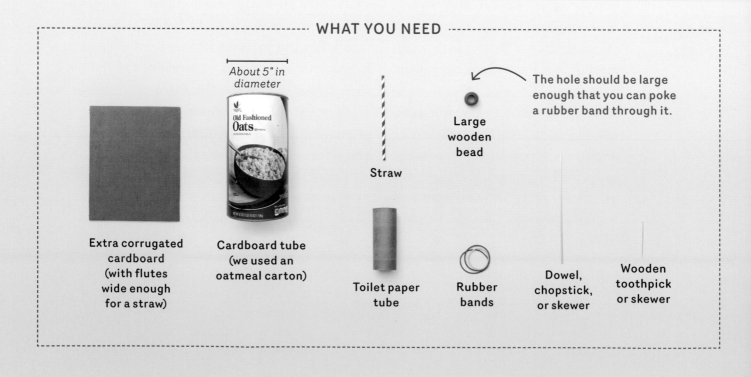

WHAT YOU NEED

Extra corrugated cardboard (with flutes wide enough for a straw)

About 5" in diameter

Cardboard tube (we used an oatmeal carton)

Old Fashioned Oats

Straw

Large wooden bead

The hole should be large enough that you can poke a rubber band through it.

Toilet paper tube

Rubber bands

Dowel, chopstick, or skewer

Wooden toothpick or skewer

ENGINEER'S BLUEPRINT

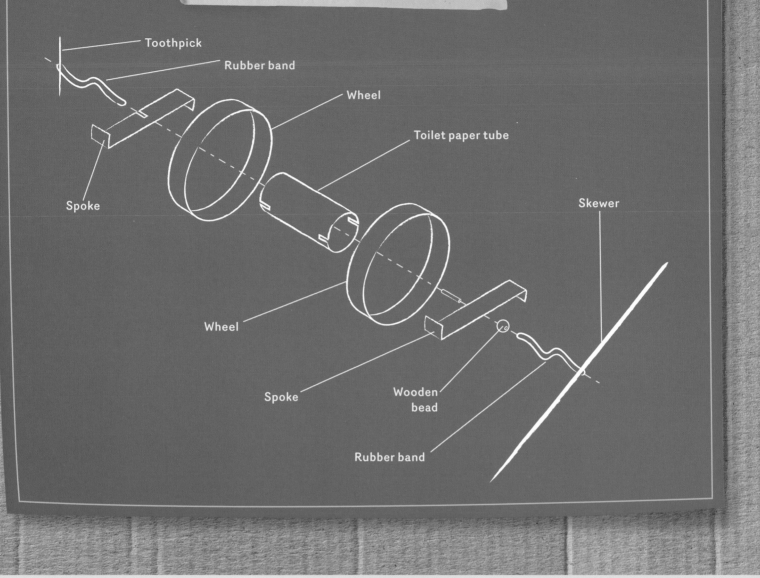

Toothpick

Rubber band

Wheel

Toilet paper tube

Spoke

Skewer

Wheel

Spoke

Wooden bead

Rubber band

WHAT'S GOING ON

Winding the rubber band creates and stores *elastic potential energy* — energy that results from twisting or pulling something springy so that it wants to spring back. Just how much energy is stored depends on the elasticity — the stretchiness — of the material you are twisting and how much you twist it. When you place the Big Wheel on the floor, the rubber band wants to untwist, and the winding stick transfers that force to the wheels, where the potential energy is converted to *kinetic energy*, the energy of motion.

A rubber band's stretchiness is its superpower.

BUILD THE WHEELS!

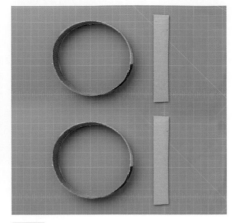

1 Cut two rings from the cardboard tube, each about 1 inch wide. Cut two strips from the corrugated cardboard, also about 1 inch wide and about 1 inch longer than the diameter of the rings (ours are 6½ inches long.)

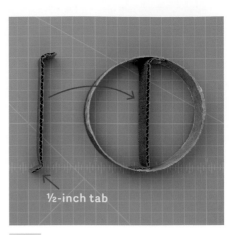

½-inch tab

2 Fold a ½-inch tab at each end of the cardboard strips. Hot-glue the strips in the center of the rings as spokes.

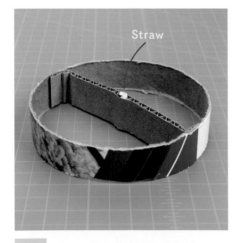

Straw

3 Use a toothpick or skewer to widen the center flute in one of the spokes. Insert the straw and cut it to fit.

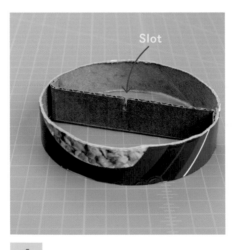

Slot

4 Cut a small slot in the center of the other spoke.

The slots should be just wide enough to fit over the corrugated cardboard.

½"

5 Cut pairs of slots in each end of the toilet paper tube, about ½ inch long and just wide enough to slip over the spokes.

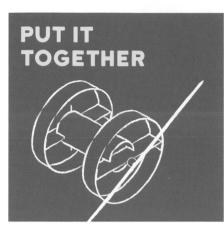

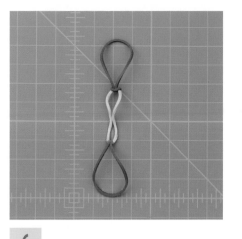

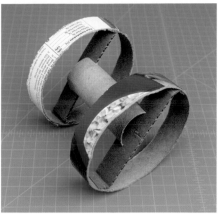

6 Loop rubber bands together (see page 73) to make a chain as long as the toilet paper tube.

7 Fit the wheel spokes into the toilet paper tube slots.

READY, SET . . .

Wind the dowel a few dozen times, then set the Big Wheel on a smooth floor and let it go.

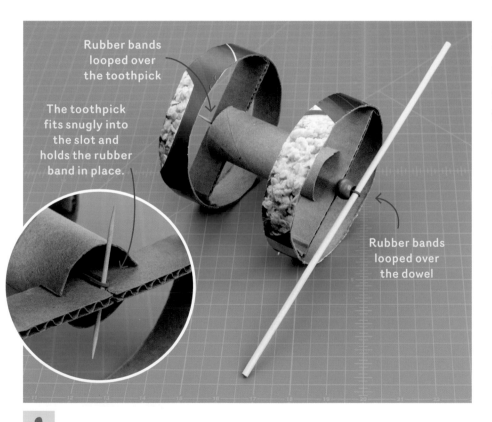

Rubber bands looped over the toothpick

The toothpick fits snugly into the slot and holds the rubber band in place.

Rubber bands looped over the dowel

8 Loop one end of the rubber-band chain around the dowel, then thread the rubber-band chain through the wooden bead. Use the toothpick to push the other end of the chain through the straw, then through the toilet paper tube and out the other side. Loop the end of the rubber band around the toothpick and slide the toothpick into the slot in the spoke, as shown.

SOLAR COOKER

If you have ever climbed into a car that's been parked in the sun on a bright summer day, you know how powerful solar heating can be. Sunlight passing through the windows makes the car's interior feel like an oven. This solar cooker works the same way: the sun's rays pass through the plastic window and the heat is trapped by the insulated walls. On a bright summer day, you can let the sun bake you up a cheese sandwich or melt a plate of s'mores — while you take a break in the shade.

Bake up a snack using the power of the sun!

WHAT YOU NEED

Cardboard file folder box with lid

ABOUT OUR BOX: It's a standard 12-inch by 15-inch file folder box with a snug-fitting lid. If you use another kind of cardboard box, make sure the lid fits tightly. If it doesn't, you can line the rim of the lid with duct tape.

Newspapers

Oven roasting bag, turkey size

Black construction paper

Heavy-duty aluminum foil

About 10"

Glue stick

Duct tape

Bendable wire (such as floral wire)

Packing tape

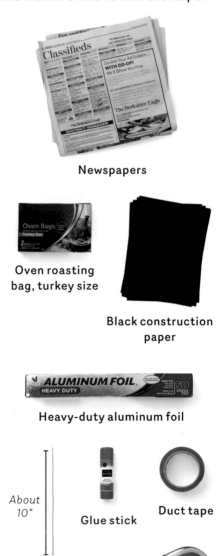

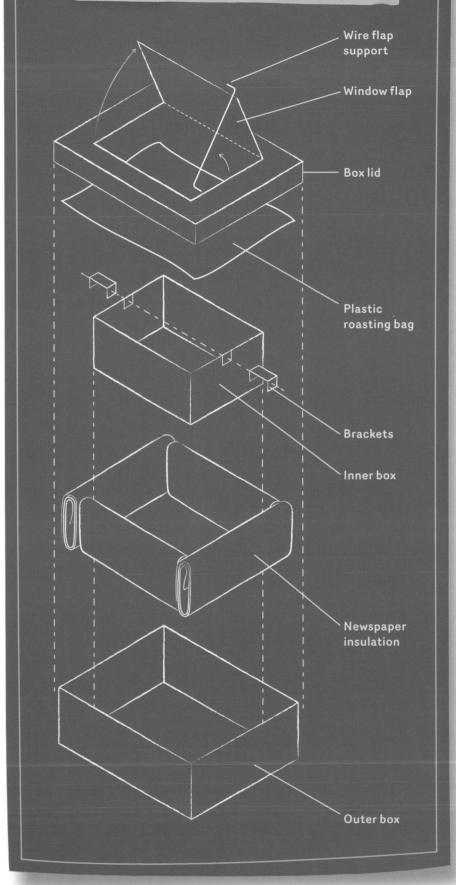

- Wire flap support
- Window flap
- Box lid
- Plastic roasting bag
- Brackets
- Inner box
- Newspaper insulation
- Outer box

CONSTRUCT THE COOKER

1 Mark around the perimeter and cut the box down so it's about 5 inches tall (a cardboard saw works well for this). Save the scrap pieces! Use packing tape to seal any holes or loose seams.

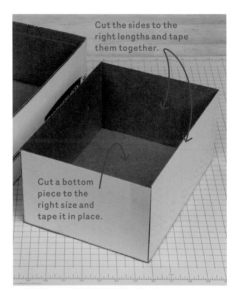

Cut the sides to the right lengths and tape them together.

Cut a bottom piece to the right size and tape it in place.

2 From the pieces of the box that you cut off, make a smaller box, a couple inches shorter on all sides and, like the first box, about 5 inches tall. Trim the sides to the right length, then tape them together, and make a bottom from other scrap pieces.

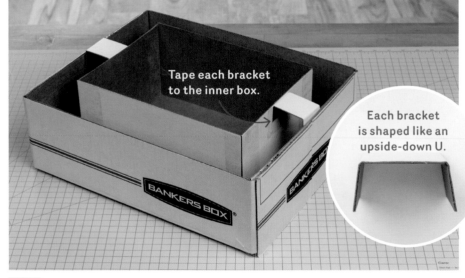

Tape each bracket to the inner box.

Each bracket is shaped like an upside-down U.

3 Set the smaller box inside the larger box, centering it. Cut and fold two U-shaped brackets from scrap cardboard to hold it in place. Tape the brackets to the sides of the inner box, as shown.

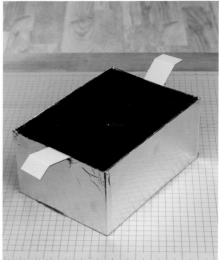

4 Line the inside of the larger box with aluminum foil, cutting pieces and gluing them in place. Cover the outside and the inside of the inner box with aluminum foil as well. Duct-tape around all of the top edges to hold everything in place, if needed.

5 Cut and glue a lining of black paper inside the smaller box.

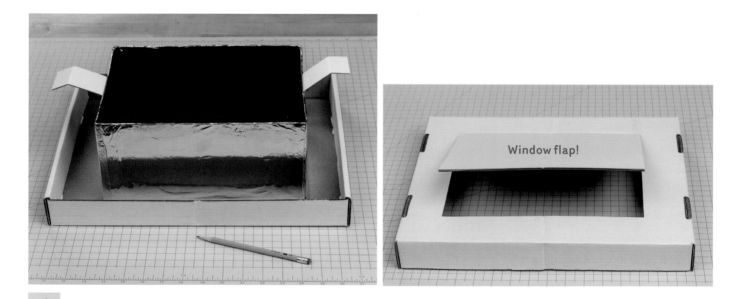

Window flap!

6 Center the smaller box on the lid and trace around it to mark the window opening. (Ours is roughly 2 inches in from each side.) Cut three sides of the window opening, leaving the fourth as a hinge for the window flap.

CONSTRUCT THE COVER

7 Measure and cut a piece of the oven roasting bag to fit over the window opening, with a few inches to spare. Cut the bag without opening it up for a double layer. Carefully tape the bag in place on the inside of the lid, making sure the bag is taut, then run tape around the bag's perimeter to seal it tightly.

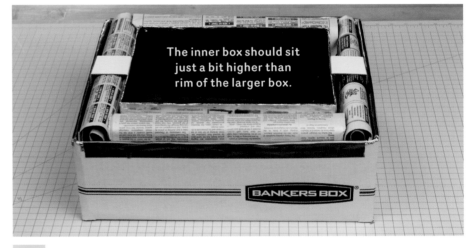

The inner box should sit just a bit higher than rim of the larger box.

8 Line the inside of the window flap with aluminum foil, gluing it in place.

9 Fold a section of newspaper into a pad about ½ inch thick and lay it on the bottom of the larger box. Then set the inner box in place. Tuck more folded newspapers between the inner and outer walls as insulation.

Take It Further

Solar ovens are used in sunny climates around the world. The designs vary, but all work by directing and capturing the sun's rays. For our window material (what an engineer would call *glazing*), we used a plastic oven bag, which doesn't melt when it gets hot (it may, however, get brittle over time). You could also try using glass or clear plastic. Our window flap is covered in aluminum foil, but you might try other reflective materials. And some cookers have four reflectors, surrounding the window. Our insulation is newspaper — cheap and available. But would another material be more effective?

Slip the ends of the wire into the flutes.

10 Create a flap support from a 10-inch piece of wire, bending each end and slipping the ends into the flutes of the lid and the flap.

COOKING WITH THE SOLAR COOKER

To use your solar cooker, you'll need a warm, sunny day. Set the food you want to cook — a cheese sandwich, say, or some marshmallow-and-chocolate s'mores — on a tray or plate inside the black box, and place the cooker in the sun, angling the window flap so that it reflects light into the hole. If you want to see how hot it can get, set an oven thermometer inside. Be patient! A cardboard solar cooker gets hot, but not as hot as the oven in your kitchen. It will take longer for your food to cook.

The sun's rays passing through the plastic bag are absorbed by the dark surface of the inner box and converted into heat. The double wall of insulation traps the heat, and over time the temperature in the cooker rises. The same forces are also at work in global warming, but instead of a plastic bag, a layer of carbon dioxide in the atmosphere is trapping the sun's energy. Scientists call this the *greenhouse effect*.

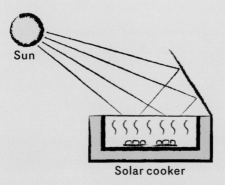

Sun

Solar cooker

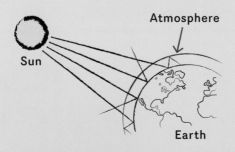

Sun

Atmosphere

Earth

The heat inside the solar cooker is similar to the phenomenon of global warming, which is explained by the greenhouse effect.

WIND-POWERED TRACTOR

It may look like a farm tractor that collided with a weather station, but this oddball contraption is no accidental mash-up. Set it outside on a breezy day and it demonstrates the power of one of our oldest energy sources: wind. The spinning cups catch the wind and turn a horizontal gear edged with toothpick cogs, which turn matching cogs on the vertical gear attached to the tractor's back wheel. The interlocking gears look like what you'd see in a a400-year-old Dutch windmill, but instead of grinding grain or pumping water, this wind-powered device uses the breeze to roll on down the road.

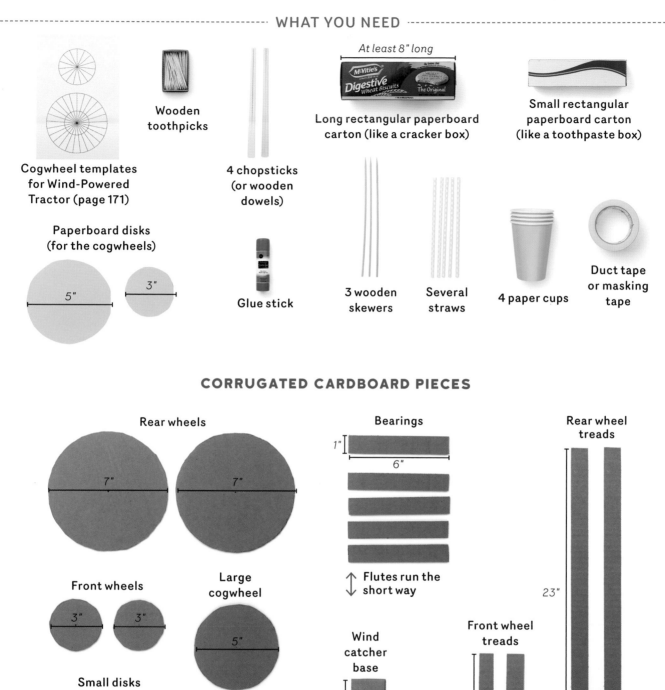

Cogwheel templates for Wind-Powered Tractor (page 171)

Wooden toothpicks

4 chopsticks (or wooden dowels)

At least 8" long

Long rectangular paperboard carton (like a cracker box)

Small rectangular paperboard carton (like a toothpaste box)

Paperboard disks (for the cogwheels)

5"

3"

Glue stick

3 wooden skewers

Several straws

4 paper cups

Duct tape or masking tape

CORRUGATED CARDBOARD PIECES

Rear wheels

7"

7"

Bearings

1"

6"

↑ Flutes run the short way ↓

Rear wheel treads

23"

Front wheels

3"

3"

Large cogwheel

5"

Small disks

1" 1" 1"

1" 1" 1"

Small cogwheel

3"

Use a compass to draw all the wheels so that each one has a hole marked at its center. (See Draw a Circle, page 19.)

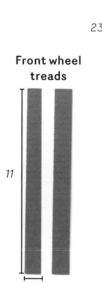

Wind catcher base

8½"

2"

Front wheel treads

11

1"

↔ Flutes run the short way

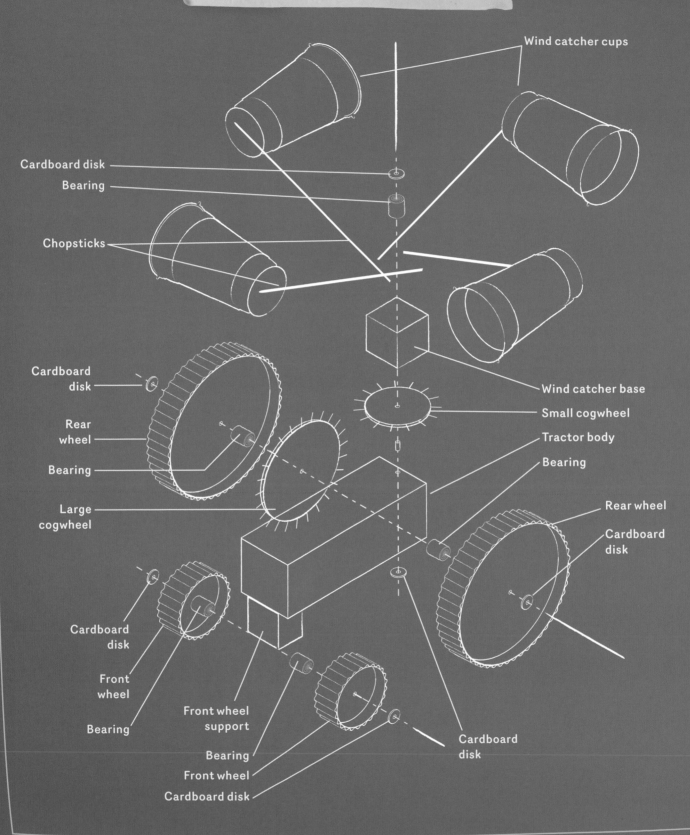

Wind catcher cups

Cardboard disk

Bearing

Chopsticks

Cardboard disk

Rear wheel

Bearing

Large cogwheel

Wind catcher base

Small cogwheel

Tractor body

Bearing

Rear wheel

Cardboard disk

Cardboard disk

Front wheel

Bearing

Front wheel support

Bearing

Front wheel

Cardboard disk

Cardboard disk

MAKE THE COGWHEELS

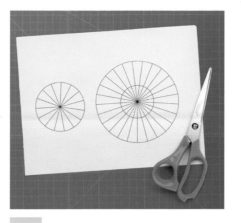

1 Cut out the circular templates for the large and small cogwheels.

2 For each cogwheel, find the side of the cardboard disk that does not have a hole marking its center. Paste the paper template to that side of the cardboard disk (be generous with the glue, applying it all the way to the edge of the wheels).

Drawing the disk with a compass leaves a hole at the center. Glue the template to the other side of the disk.

On the large cogwheel, align the tip of each toothpick with the inner circle.

On the small cogwheel, align the tip of each toothpick around the outside of the mark for the center hole.

3 Run a line of hot glue along each line on the cogwheel templates, then set toothpicks in place, as shown.

Note: We used hot glue because it dries quickly, but white glue would also work.

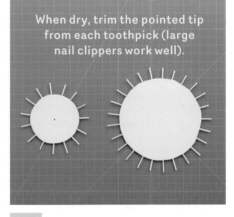

When dry, trim the pointed tip from each toothpick (large nail clippers work well).

4 Apply a generous spiral of glue over the toothpicks. Then press the paperboard circles on top, sandwiching the toothpicks between the cardboard and the paperboard. Set a book or other flat weight on top of the cogwheels until the glue is dry.

MAKE THE TRACTOR WHEELS

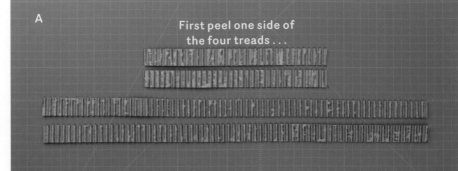

A

First peel one side of
the four treads . . .

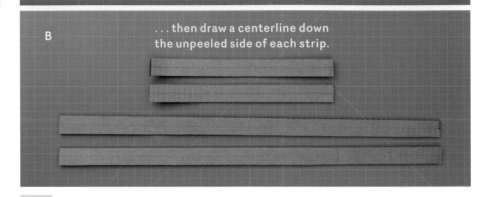

B

. . . then draw a centerline down
the unpeeled side of each strip.

5 Using the Peeling Corrugated Cardboard technique (page 21), peel the linerboard from one side of the tread strips (A). Then flip them over and draw a line down the center of each strip on the unpeeled side (B).

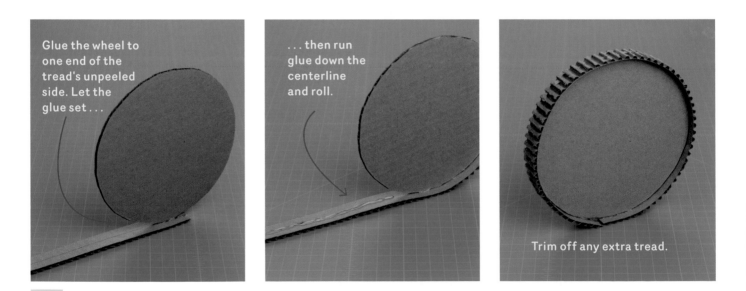

Glue the wheel to one end of the tread's unpeeled side. Let the glue set . . .

. . . then run glue down the centerline and roll.

Trim off any extra tread.

6 Hot-glue the treads onto each of the four wheels using the rolling technique shown here.

Glue each bearing around a length of straw...

...then trim the straws to fit.

7 Using the Roll a Bearing technique (page 18), roll five bearings from the 1- by 6-inch cardboard strips and the straws.

NOTE: If you're using paper straws, be careful not to crush them as you're rolling the bearings.

ENGINEER SPOTLIGHT: THEO JANSEN

Artist and engineer Theo Jansen (born in 1948) lives near the ocean in Holland, the country whose windmills made wind power famous, but his amazing creations are like no windmill you've ever seen. Assembled from hundreds of pieces of PVC pipe, combined with various hinges, joints, plastic bottles, tubes, sails, and wires, these *strandbeesten* (Dutch for "beach beasts") come to life when the breeze blows, walking across the sand on dozens of mechanical legs like giant insect robots.

Jansen began his work nearly 30 years ago and has been engineering new and more elaborate strandbeests ever since. He exhibits his creatures at art museums and science centers all over the world. "Eventually," he says, "I want to put these animals out in herds on the beaches, so they will live their own lives." To see them in action, search for "strandbeest" on YouTube.

Jansen on the beach with Animaris Plaudens Vela, a wind-powered strandbeest, created in 2013.

ASSEMBLE THE WHEELS

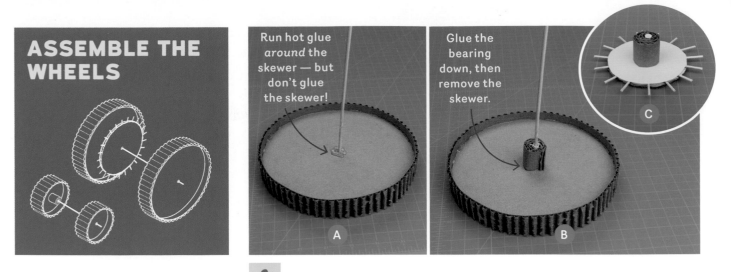

Run hot glue *around* the skewer — but don't glue the skewer! **A**

Glue the bearing down, then remove the skewer. **B**

C

8 Insert a skewer through the center of a wheel, at the point made by the compass, to serve as a guide for gluing on a bearing. Run a line of hot glue around the skewer, as shown (A). Slide a bearing onto the skewer and press it down onto the wheel (B). Then remove the skewer. Repeat for the other three wheels. Do the same for the smaller cogwheel, being sure to glue the bearing to the front of the cogwheel, on the paperboard (C).

Apply glue here, avoiding the straw in the middle.

9 Slide the larger cogwheel onto a skewer. Run a line of hot glue around the top of one of the rear-wheel bearings, insert the skewer into the bearing, and press the cogwheel into place, sandwiching the bearing between the cogwheel and the rear wheel. Then remove the skewer.

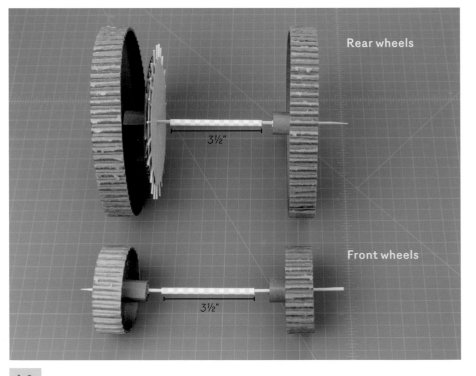

Rear wheels

3½"

Front wheels

3½"

10 Assemble each set of wheels on a skewer, threading the skewer first through a wheel with a bearing, then a 3½-inch length of straw, and finally the other wheel.

INSTALL THE SMALL COGWHEEL

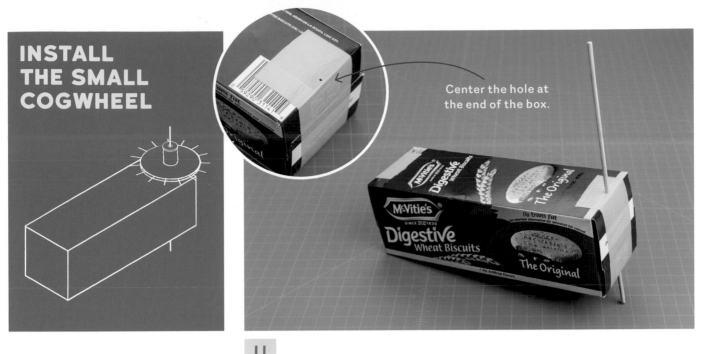

Center the hole at the end of the box.

11 Tape the ends of the cracker box. Using the Pushpin Puncture technique (page 22), make holes at the very end of the cracker box and insert a skewer, as shown.

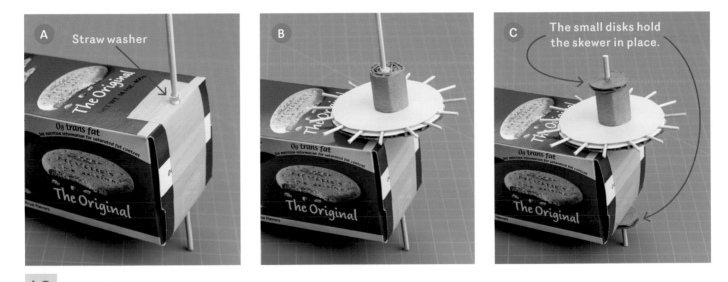

A Straw washer

B

C The small disks hold the skewer in place.

12 Thread the ⅛-inch piece of straw onto the skewer as a washer (A). Then slide on the small cogwheel (B). Use a pushpin to poke a hole in two of the 1-inch cardboard disks, and then slide them onto the ends of the skewer to hold it in place. Trim the skewer, leaving about an inch extending on the top and bottom (C).

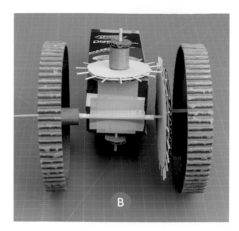

ATTACH THE WHEELS

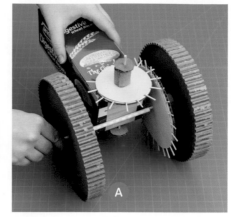

A

B

13 Hold the rear wheel assembly against the back of the cracker box and slide it up until the cogs (the toothpicks) on the two cogwheels meet (A). Tape the straw to the box at that location (B). Then test the cogwheel mechanism: when you turn the top cogwheel, the toothpicks should weave into the toothpicks on the larger cogwheel, so that the two spin smoothly in unison. Adjust the position of the rear wheel assembly if needed.

Cut along the dotted lines to make flaps.

1"

3"

A

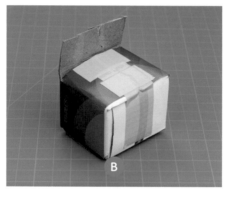

B

14 Cut off a 3-inch section of toothpaste box and slice down the corners to create 1-inch flaps (A). Fold in three of the flaps and tape them in place (B).

15 Hot-glue the box to the front of the tractor, as shown.

Make sure the tractor body is level.

If the skewers are long or pointy, trim them.

16 Tape the front wheel assembly to the box. You can attach it to the bottom or the front of the box — whichever keeps the tractor level.

17 Poke a hole in the four remaining 1-inch disks, then slide them onto the front- and rear-wheel skewers to hold everything in place.

MAKE THE WIND CATCHER

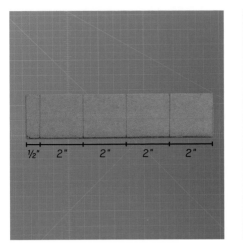

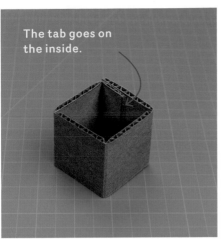

The tab goes on the inside.

18 To make the wind catcher base, mark fold lines on the 8½-by-2-inch strip of cardboard, as shown above. Then fold the cardboard into a 2-inch square, hot-gluing the ½-inch tab on the inside of the square to secure it.

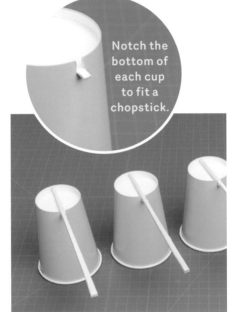

Notch the bottom of each cup to fit a chopstick.

19 If the cups are waxy, sand the bottoms with sandpaper. Cut a notch in each, as shown. Then hot-glue the ends of the chopsticks across the bottom of the cups.

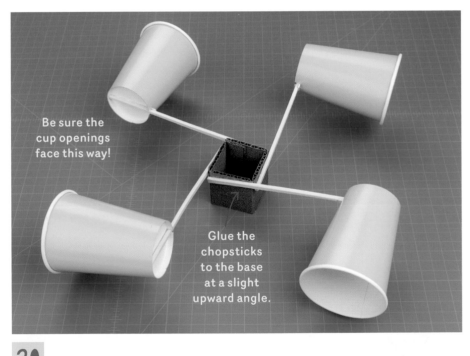

Be sure the cup openings face this way!

Glue the chopsticks to the base at a slight upward angle.

20 Hot-glue the chopsticks to the base frame at a slight upward angle, making sure the cup openings face clockwise (so that the wind catcher turns counterclockwise).

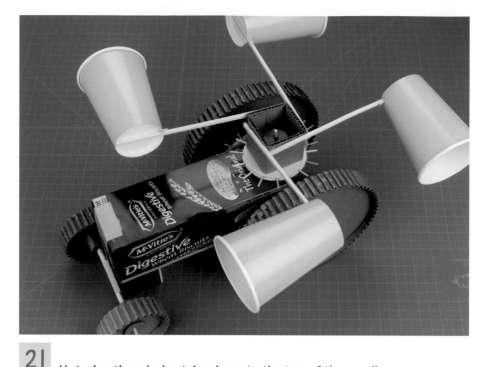

Turn the wind catcher by hand to see how the cogs are working. If they bind, adjust the position of the rear wheels and other parts, or trim the toothpick cogs. Take the tractor outside, place it on a hard, flat surface, and wait for the wind to blow. On a still day, create your own wind by fanning the tractor with a large sheet of cardboard.

21 Hot-glue the wind catcher base to the top of the small cogwheel, over the bearing, as shown.

SPEAK LIKE AN ENGINEER

Wind-powered devices come in many forms. The spinning cups on our Wind-Powered Tractor resemble the scientific tool called an *anemometer* (A), which is used to measure wind speed. Large propeller-shaped windmills that generate electricity are called *wind turbines* (B). A *Savonius turbine* (C) has upright scoops that form an S shape when viewed from above.

CHAPTER 7

SERIOUS FUN

GAME DESIGN

A well-designed game is easy to learn but difficult to master. It challenges you, tests your skills, and forces you to think — but it never stops being fun. To achieve this, game designers have to consider the game's appearance, the rules and goals, how much luck or strategy is needed to win, and any other factor that could affect the player's experience. Because the best board and video games have a distinctive look, creating them requires both engineering and artistic skills.

Video game designers also need more specialized knowledge, such as computer programming and graphic design skills, which are now taught at many colleges and universities. But as complex as engineering a game may be, the final product still has to have that magical mix of challenge and fun that keeps us coming back for more. A game made from cardboard can do the same, as the following projects reveal.

TABLETOP STRAW SOCCER

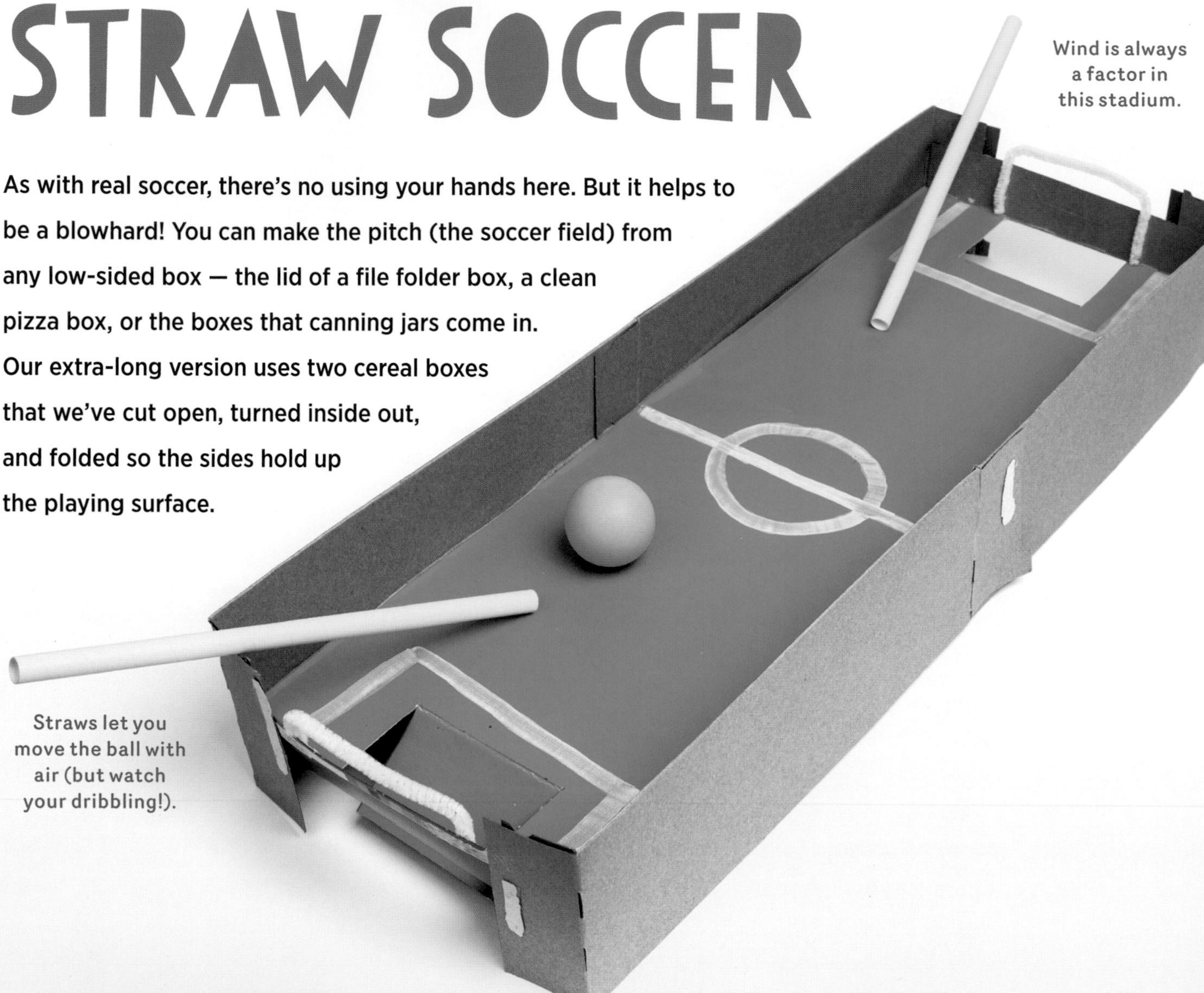

Wind is always a factor in this stadium.

As with real soccer, there's no using your hands here. But it helps to be a blowhard! You can make the pitch (the soccer field) from any low-sided box — the lid of a file folder box, a clean pizza box, or the boxes that canning jars come in. Our extra-long version uses two cereal boxes that we've cut open, turned inside out, and folded so the sides hold up the playing surface.

Straws let you move the ball with air (but watch your dribbling!).

WHAT YOU NEED

2 cereal boxes of the same size

Green paper or cardstock

2 white pipe cleaners (optional)

Straws

Ping-Pong ball

Glue stick

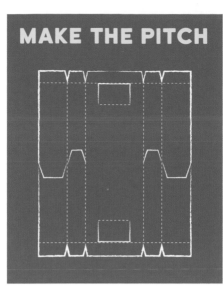

MAKE THE PITCH

1 Carefully separate all the glued flaps on the top and bottom of both cereal boxes. Measure and draw a line down the center of each box's front panel. Use scissors to cut each front panel along the line.

Interweave the flaps.

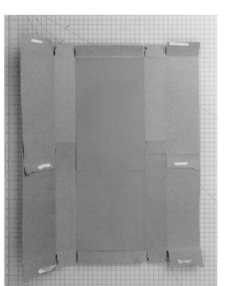

Don't cut this edge! Instead, fold it down to make a flap.

2 Fit the two boxes together to form one long open box, interweaving and trimming the flaps in the middle as needed. Hot-glue the two boxes together.

3 Measure and cut green paper to cover the center panel of the boxes. Use a glue stick to paste it in place.

4 Make a goal at each end of the joined boxes by using a knife to cut a rectangular flap in the green playing field. Our goals are 2 inches by 3 inches.

ASSEMBLE THE FIELD

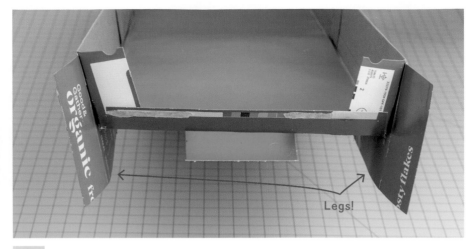

Legs!

5 Fold down the pieces that used to be the front panels of the boxes. Glue them to the side panels, forming legs.

ENGINEER SPOTLIGHT: SHIGERU MIYAMOTO

If you've ever played a Nintendo video game, chances are you know the work of Shigeru Miyamoto (born in 1952), who is often called the Walt Disney of video game design. His groundbreaking approach — using characters and telling stories — made video games such as Super Mario Brothers, The Legend of Zelda, and Star Fox among the most popular of all time.

As a boy, Shigeru enjoyed exploring the forests and caves near his home in Japan, and his games share this love of nature and the thrill of discovery. When he was in college studying industrial design, video games had not yet been invented. Shigeru drew comics, painted, and created homemade toys. His first success at Nintendo was in 1981 with Donkey Kong, an arcade game that marked the beginning of the company's — and Shigeru's — rise to the top of the video game industry.

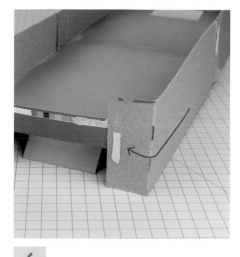

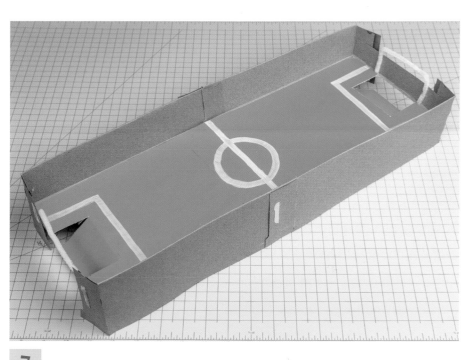

6 Glue the end flaps to enclose the playing field, as shown.

7 Draw field lines with a marker or white tape. If you like, measure and cut pipe cleaners for goalposts and glue them in place.

HOW TO PLAY

Place the Ping-Pong ball in the center of the field. Use a straw to try to blow it into your opponent's goal hole. Use extra-long straws for more challenging action.

CHAIN REACTION

The classic board game Mouse Trap proves that chain reactions just never get old. Even after 50 years, we still get a kick out of taking a bunch of wacky plastic game pieces — a stop sign, swinging boot, old bathtub, rickety staircase, rain gutter, rattly cage — and engineering them into a ridiculously complex rodent catcher. Today, you can see this same idea taken to a room-size level by searching for "chain reactions" on YouTube. The elaborate Rube Goldberg–style contraptions you'll find there can seem magical, but they are really demonstrations of physics — the science of how things move. Many chain reactions rely on simple machines, the earliest tools of engineering: the lever, wheel and axle, pulley, inclined plane, wedge, and screw. But simple components can be combined into complex mechanisms, as this cardboard version demonstrates. And don't feel limited to the design shown here. In this game, winning is all about unleashing your imagination — as well as the forces of nature.

ENGINEER SPOTLIGHT: RUBE GOLDBERG

Rube Goldberg (1883–1970) was trained as an engineer, but he became famous for his cartoons of hilariously complicated chain-reaction gadgets that do simple tasks, like a self-operating napkin. His work — often featuring a Professor Lucifer Gorgonzola Butts — appeared in newspapers around the country, as well as in films and books. He won the Pulitzer Prize for his cartoons in 1948 and his name became an adjective in dictionaries, a way to describe something made overly complicated. Goldberg's work has inspired a number of engineering contests where teams compete to create the most impressive chain-reaction contraptions. Professor Butts would be proud.

The self-operating napkin is really very simple, as Rube Goldberg explained it: "As you raise spoon of soup (A) to your mouth it pulls string (B), thereby jerking ladle (C) which throws cracker (D) past parrot (E). Parrot jumps after cracker and perch (F) tilts, upsetting seeds (G) into pail (H). Extra weight in pail pulls cord (I) which opens and lights automatic cigar lighter (J), setting off sky-rocket (K) which causes sickle (L) to cut string (M) and allow pendulum with attached napkin to swing back and forth thereby wiping off your chin."

STATION #1
The Marble Plunge

Start the reaction by sending a marble down the paper plate track and into the swinging arm. The arm drops the marble into the outlet tube, which sends it . . .

STATION #4
The Victory Sign

. . . and topples the tube tower, which is holding up a tennis ball. The falling ball, with the help of a pulley, hoists the victory sign. Success!

STATION #3
The Wrecking Ball

. . . and when the last box tumbles, it yanks out the wedge, which releases the golf ball. The ball rolls down the inclined plane, picking up speed . . .

STATION #2
Cereal Box Dominoes

. . . flying off the bounce pad into the first box in the row of cereal boxes. They fall like dominoes . . .

STATION 1: THE MARBLE PLUNGE

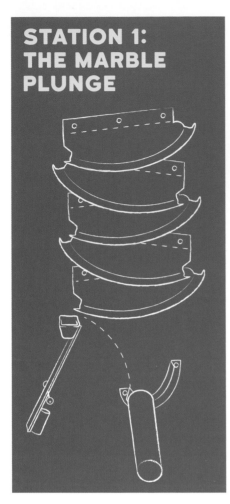

Tinker with the parts until a marble rolls down the plates, falls into the swinging arm, and gets dropped into the outlet tube.

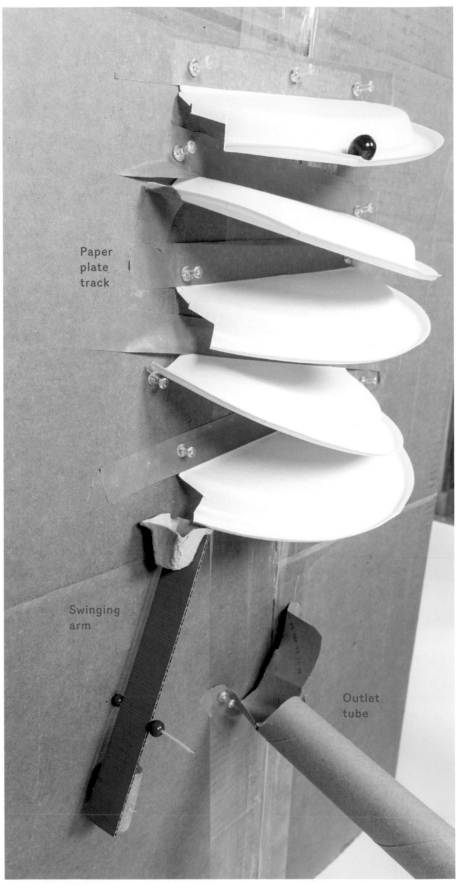

Paper plate track

Swinging arm

Outlet tube

Attach the plates to the wall in a stack, as shown, using tape and pushpins. Alternate the notched plates, and tilt them so that the marble zigzags down your ramp. This will take tinkering!

The swinging arm deposits the marble in the tube, which drops it onto the bounce pad (see Station 2).

Align the notch in the last track piece with the cup at the top of the swinging arm.

SWINGING ARM

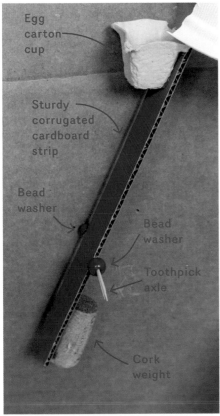

Egg carton cup

Sturdy corrugated cardboard strip

Bead washer

Bead washer

Toothpick axle

Cork weight

Insert the toothpick through the flutes of your cardboard strip, glue beads on either side, and poke the toothpick into the cardboard box to pin the swinging arm in place.

OUTLET TUBE

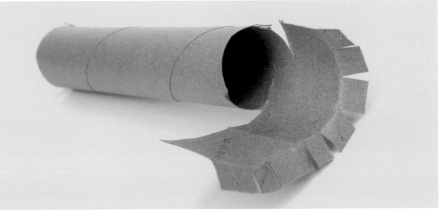

Cut open the end of a paper towel tube, as shown. Snip tabs so you can tape and pin the tube to the cardboard box.

PAPER PLATE TRACK

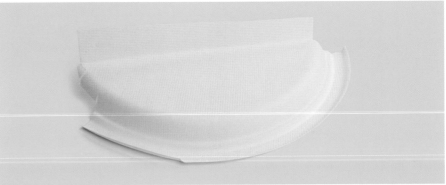

Cut several paper plates in half, then trim each, as shown, to create a folded tab that lets you attach it to the box. Cut notches in the rim so that the marble drops down to the plate beneath it. Notch half the plates on one side, half on the other.

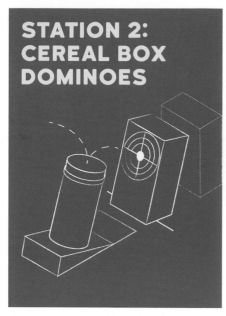

STATION 2: CEREAL BOX DOMINOES

After launching off the bounce pad, the marble topples the row of cereal boxes. When the last box falls, it tugs on a length of string attached to a wedge, which releases the golf ball in Station 3.

End the row with a tall box, and tape a length of string to the top.

Set up the boxes in a row. The spacing will depend on the size of your boxes. It may take a little tinkering to get it right.

Use as many boxes as you like!

Try pasting a target to the first box.

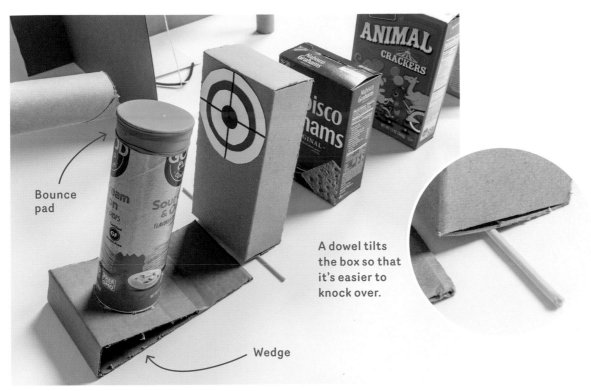

Bounce pad

A dowel tilts the box so that it's easier to knock over.

Wedge

Set up the first box so that the marble will bounce off the bounce pad, hit the box, and knock it over. If the box doesn't fall, set a dowel under it to tilt it.

BOUNCE PAD

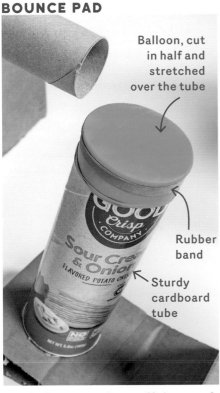

Balloon, cut in half and stretched over the tube

Rubber band

Sturdy cardboard tube

For the bounce pad, cut off the top of a balloon, stretch it over a potato chip tube (or a similar sturdy container), and secure it with a rubber band.

WEDGE

Set your bounce pad on a cardboard wedge to launch the marble toward the cereal boxes. Fold and tape the corrugated cardboard as shown.

STRING TRIGGER

Tape a length of string to the top of the last box. When the box topples, it will pull the string.

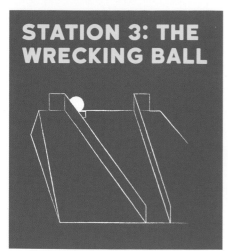

STATION 3: THE WRECKING BALL

Adjust the position of the last cereal box so that when it falls, it pulls out the wedge, releasing the golf ball.

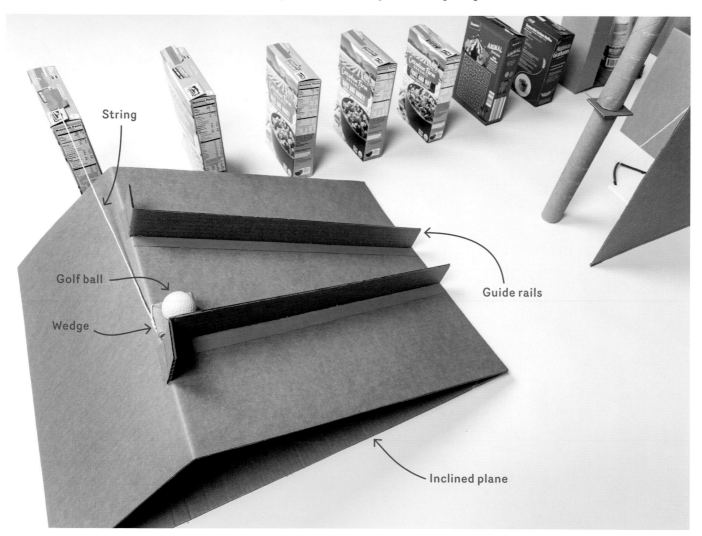

String

Golf ball

Wedge

Guide rails

Inclined plane

INCLINED PLANE

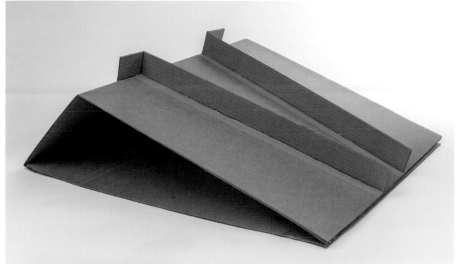

Fold a large sheet of corrugated cardboard into an inclined plane, as shown. Tape or glue the ends together, if necessary, to secure them. Tape two long strips of cardboard on top, in a V shape, to direct the path of the golf ball.

WEDGE

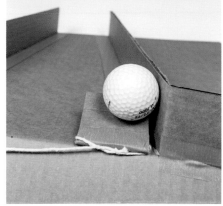

Fold and tape another cardboard wedge to hold the golf ball. Loop the end of the string from the last cereal-box domino through the wedge, as shown, and tie it.

RAILS

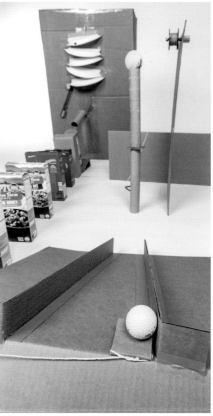

The rails guide the golf ball toward its target in Station 4.

WHAT'S GOING ON

Simple machines were first identified by the ancient Greek engineer Archimedes and then explained mathematically by the Italian scientist Galileo Galilei (of telescope fame) in 1600. All simple machines are devices that make work easier, and to an engineer, *work* is the amount of energy it takes to move an object. An inclined plane is a simple machine, and in our Station 3, it lets us control a rolling ball more easily. A pulley, like the one in Station 4, makes it easier to lift things.

Another principle of physics at work here is *potential energy*. Placing the golf ball at the top of the inclined plane in Station 3 and resting the tennis ball on the tube tower in Station 4 loads each ball with gravitational potential energy. When the balls are knocked loose, their potential energy is transformed into kinetic energy (or motion). Likewise, the cardboard-box dominoes in Station 2 have potential energy when they are upright, which becomes kinetic energy when they fall. (For more details on these different types of energy, see page 99.) The use of potential energy, along with the power of simple machines, allows one small marble to cause a dramatic chain reaction.

STATION 4: THE VICTORY SIGN

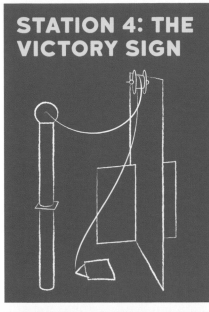

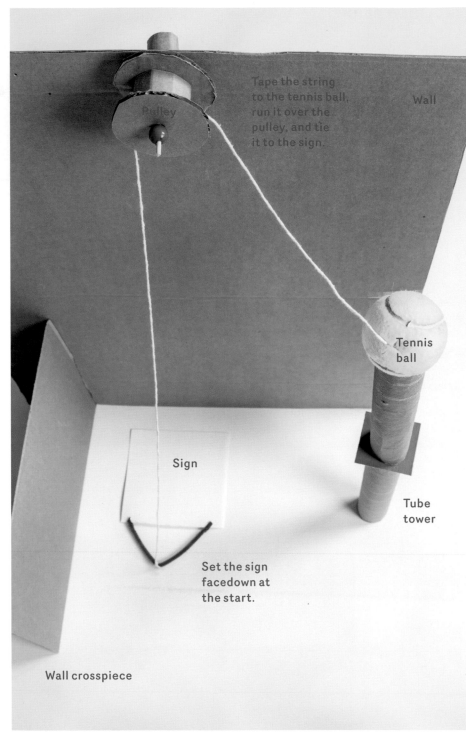

Tape the string to the tennis ball, run it over the pulley, and tie it to the sign.

Pulley

Wall

Tennis ball

Sign

Set the sign facedown at the start.

Tube tower

Wall crosspiece

When the golf ball knocks over the tube tower, the tennis ball falls, pulling the string over the pulley . . .

Make a sign from paper and a pipe cleaner, and write a victory message on the front.

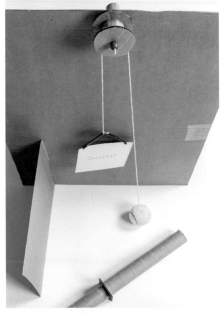

. . . and hoisting the sign for all to see!

PULLEY

To make the pulley, use the Roll a Bearing technique (page 18) to roll and glue a cardboard handle to the end of a skewer. Make a bearing using the same technique, rolling and gluing the cardboard around a straw. Hot-glue two slightly bigger disks to each side of the bearing. Push the skewer through the cardboard wall, hot-gluing its handle to the back of the wall. On the front of the wall, thread a bead over the skewer, followed by the bearing. Hot-glue the last bead to the skewer, as shown.

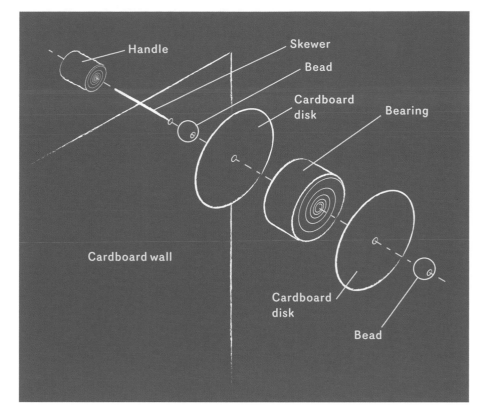

Handle · Skewer · Bead · Cardboard disk · Bearing · Cardboard wall · Cardboard disk · Bead

TOWER

Make a tube tower by stacking two paper towel tubes with a square of cardboard between them. You can tape or glue the tubes together if they won't stand.

WALL

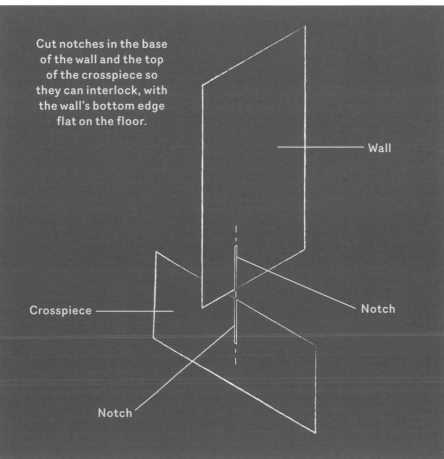

Cut notches in the base of the wall and the top of the crosspiece so they can interlock, with the wall's bottom edge flat on the floor.

Wall · Crosspiece · Notch · Notch

BOUNCY SKEE BALL

Playing competitive games requires keeping score. How else can you prove to your friends that you are, in fact, the greatest of all time? This clever target game is engineered to give you those bragging rights. Bounce a marble off the trampoline and through a hole in the target, and a hidden track drops it straight into a scoring rack. Add up the marbles in each rack to get your new high score.

Bounce your marbles off the balloon trampoline, aiming for the bull's-eye!

Marble alleys help you keep score.

Rectangular
corrugated box

*About
10–12"*

Corrugated
cardboard

Short, sturdy
cardboard container
(like a can for nuts)

12-inch
balloon

Wide rubber
bands

2 clothespins
or other clips

Packing
tape

3 nickels

Marbles

Toothpicks

PREPARE THE BOX

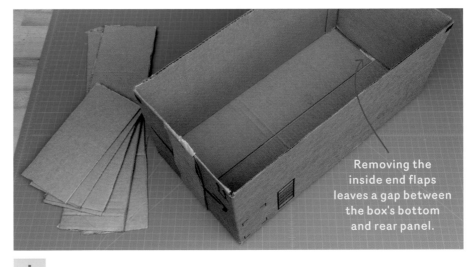

Removing the
inside end flaps
leaves a gap between
the box's bottom
and rear panel.

1 Cut the four top flaps and the two inside bottom end flaps from the box. Save the flaps.

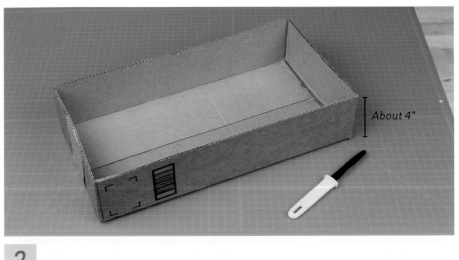

About 4"

2 Trim the box down to about 4 inches in height. Again, save any scrap pieces.

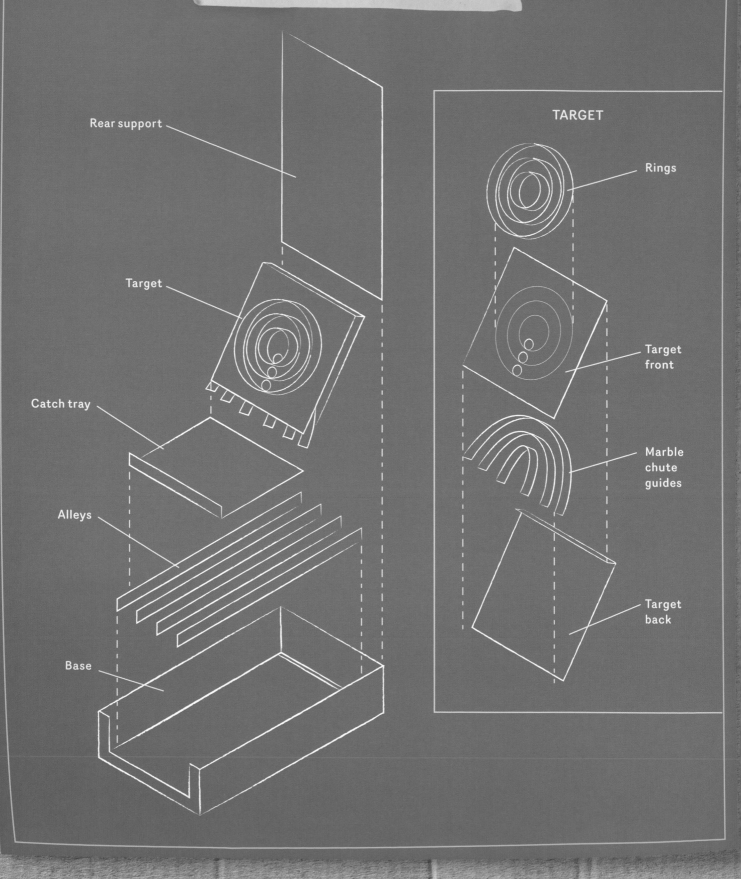

Rear support

Target

Catch tray

Alleys

Base

TARGET

Rings

Target front

Marble chute guides

Target back

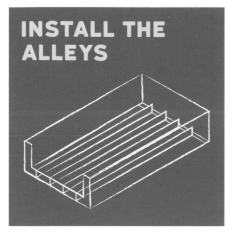

INSTALL THE ALLEYS

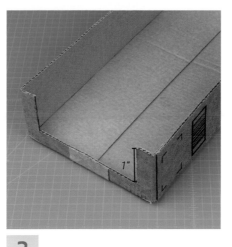

3 Cut a wide notch in the front of the box to create a 1-inch-tall front wall.

Rear support panel

4 From a sheet of cardboard or flaps that you've taped together, make a rear support panel that fits snugly into the back of the box, as shown. Slide the support panel between the bottom and rear panel of the box. If it won't stand up on its own, clip it in place with clothespins.

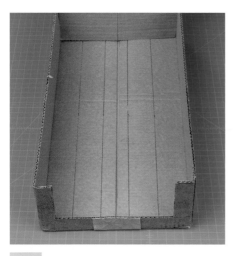

5 Measure the inside width of the box and divide by 5 to get the width of the marble alleys. Using a ruler and pencil, measure and draw four lines on the bottom of the box to mark the five alleys.

6 Measure the inside length of the box, and cut (or tape together) four 1-inch-wide strips of cardboard to fit. Hot-glue the strips in place along the marked lines.

7 Label the alleys with whatever point values you would like. The highest should be on the two outside alleys (which both connect to the bull's eye) and the lowest on the single alley in the center.

MAKE THE TARGET

NOTE: If you want to give your corrugated cardboard rings a smoother curve, peel off the linerboard on the outer side using the Peeling Corrugated Cardboard technique (page 21).

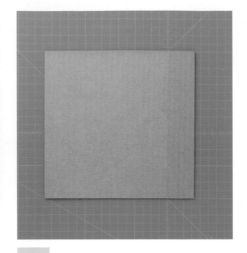

8 For the front of the target, cut a cardboard square the same width as the box.

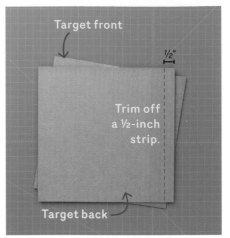

Target front

Trim off a ½-inch strip.

Target back

9 For the target back, cut another square the same size, then trim a ½-inch strip from one side.

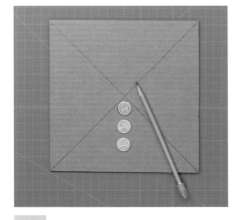

10 Draw two diagonal lines across the target front, from corner to corner. Set three nickels in a line running down from the X, spacing them about an inch apart, as shown. Trace around them to mark the target holes.

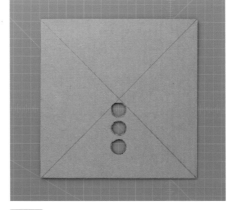

11 Use a craft knife to cut out the holes.

Draw the circles starting from the bottom edge of each hole.

12 Use a compass to draw circles for the target rings, as shown.

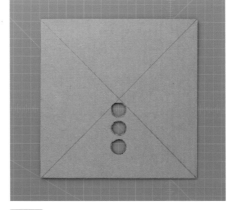

13 Cut 1-inch-wide strips of cardboard, with the flutes running the short way. Tape them into rings matching the circles on the target front.

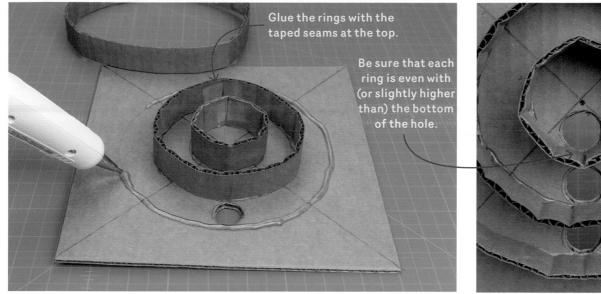

Glue the rings with the taped seams at the top.

Be sure that each ring is even with (or slightly higher than) the bottom of the hole.

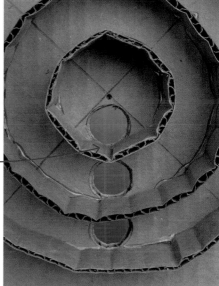

14 Hot-glue the rings in place.

Take It Further

To give your target a more finished look, use rings sliced from cardboard canisters and tubes. The rings shown here come from an oatmeal canister, a potato chip canister, and a toilet paper tube (snipped and taped so it's a bit smaller). To cut rings evenly, use painter's tape as a guide: wrap a strip around the tube and cut along the edges.

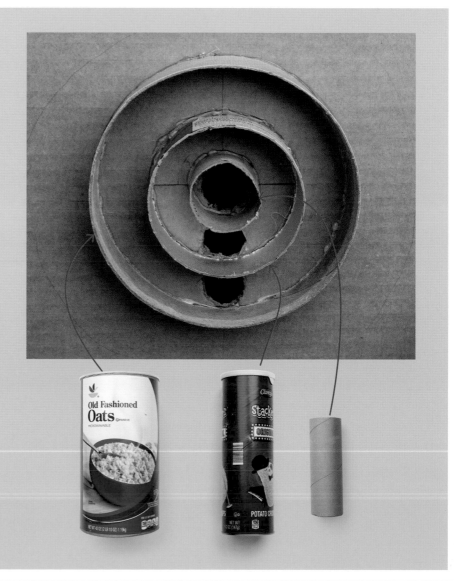

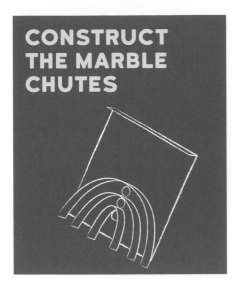

CONSTRUCT THE MARBLE CHUTES

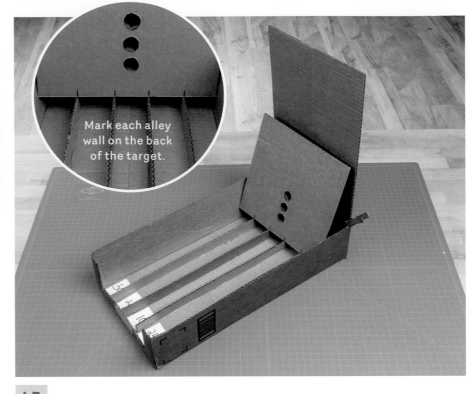

Mark each alley wall on the back of the target.

15 Set the target backward on the base, with the ring side against the rear support. Mark the location of each alley wall.

16 Cut three 1-inch-wide strips of cardboard, each about 1 foot long, with flutes running the short way. Curl them into horseshoe shapes and then hot-glue them to the back of the target, as shown. Trim the ends, leaving about an inch of overhang at the bottom.

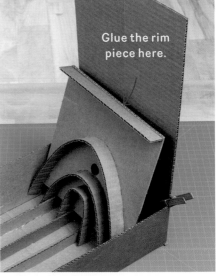

Glue the rim piece here.

17 Cut another 1-inch-wide strip and hot-glue it across the top of the target back, making a rim.

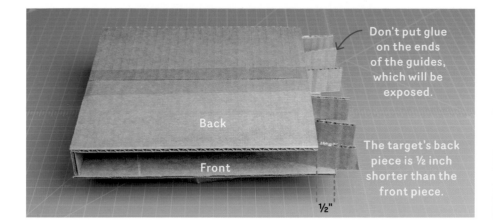

Don't put glue on the ends of the guides, which will be exposed.

The target's back piece is ½ inch shorter than the front piece.

Back

Front

½"

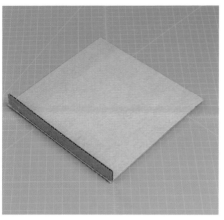

18 Run a line of hot glue along the edge of the rim and at least one of the horseshoe-shaped guides, stopping a couple inches from the end. Align the target back piece with the rim and press it in place, enclosing the guides.

19 To make a catch tray for missed shots, cut a sheet of cardboard as wide as the box and roughly half as long, and glue a 1-inch-wide strip along one edge, as shown.

If the base slips down on the rear support panel, insert toothpicks into the support's flutes to secure it.

20 Set the target and catch tray in place on the base. To give the base a bit of a forward-leaning angle, push the rear support panel down through the gap at the end of the box.

MAKE THE BOUNCE PAD

Note: If you don't have a small container for your bounce pad, you can cut a tall one, like a potato chip cannister, to roughly 3 inches tall.

21 Find a short, sturdy container to serve as the base for your bounce pad. Blow up a balloon to stretch it, then let it deflate. Cut off the top half.

22 Stretch the top half of the balloon over the mouth of the container. Secure it with a wide rubber band.

ENGINEER SPOTLIGHT: CAINE MONROY

In 2012, when Caine Monroy was 9 years old, he spent the entire summer building an elaborate arcade out of cardboard in his father's auto parts store in East Los Angeles. Using boxes from the store, he engineered versions of all his favorite games, some of which even gave out tickets that could be redeemed for prizes. The only trouble was, he had no customers.

Then Nirvan Mullick came across the arcade while looking for a part for his car. Nirvan loved arcade games, and he also happened to be a filmmaker. He made a short video about Caine, which showed Caine's reaction to the surprise flash mob Nirvan organized to generate customers. The video went viral and Caine's arcade got national attention.

In the years since, Caine has traveled around the world to share his story, inspired millions, and seen his college fund grow exponentially (he plans to study engineering or game design). Nirvan helped form the nonprofit Imagination.org, which now sponsors the Global Cardboard Challenge, a celebration of cardboard engineering and creativity. To learn more, and to see the original video, visit the Imagination.org website.

TEST AND TINKER

Set the bounce pad on the edge of the catch tray, as shown below, and test the action. Toss the marbles off the pad at an angle so they arc into the target holes. Tinker with the angle of the can and your tossing technique until you get the marble trajectory you like.

You can also adjust the position of the rear support to raise the target's height, or you can shift the angle of the target to better catch the marbles. If the catch tray slides down, insert a couple of toothpicks into the alley walls to hold it in place.

Once you have the setup you like, it's time to play! Choose an equal number of marbles for each player. Take turns as the marble tosser. After a set number of rounds, the person with the most points wins!

Insert toothpicks into the alley walls to hold the catch tray in place.

TEMPLATES

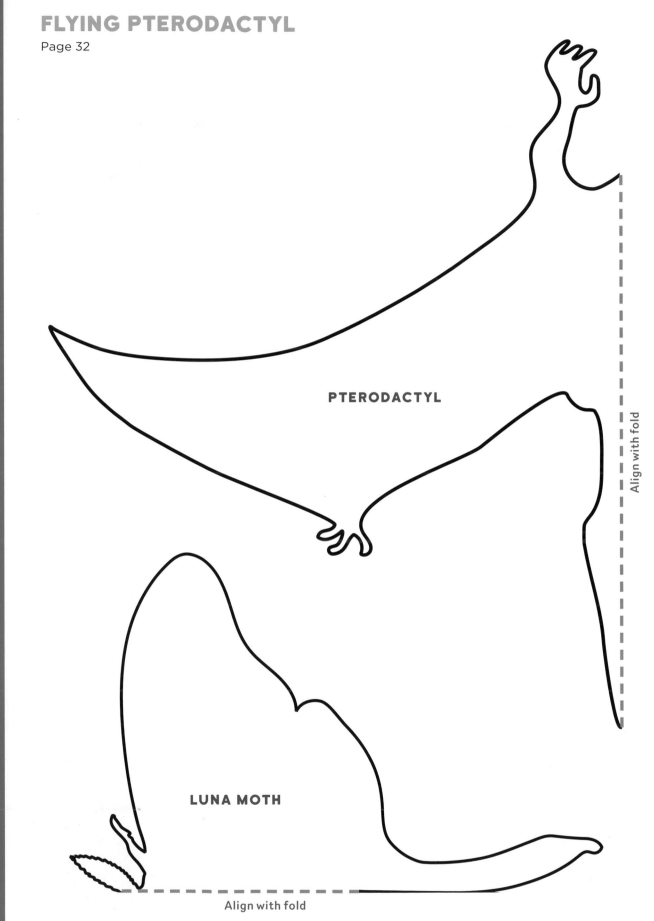

PTERODACTYL

Align with fold

LUNA MOTH

Align with fold

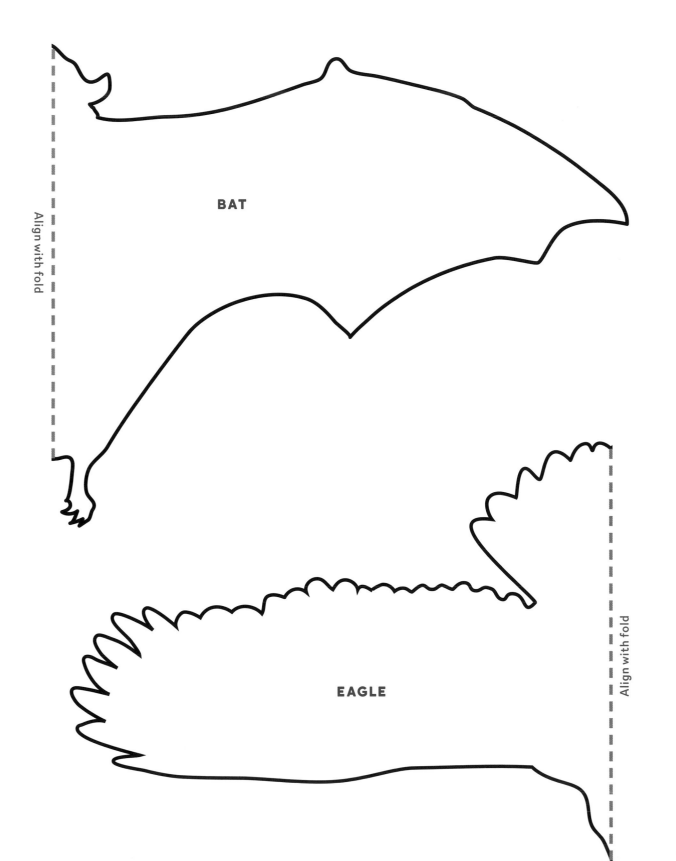

BAT

EAGLE

TEMPLATES

SWINGING MONKEY

Page 40

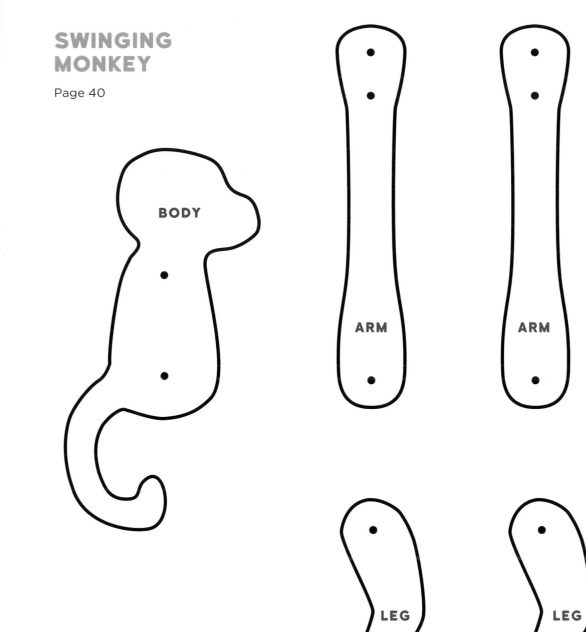

BODY

ARM

ARM

LEG

LEG

TEMPLATES

FLOATING HUMMINGBIRD

Page 90

WIND-POWERED TRACTOR

Page 130

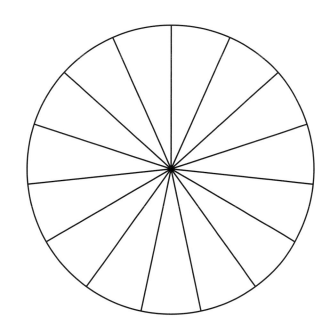

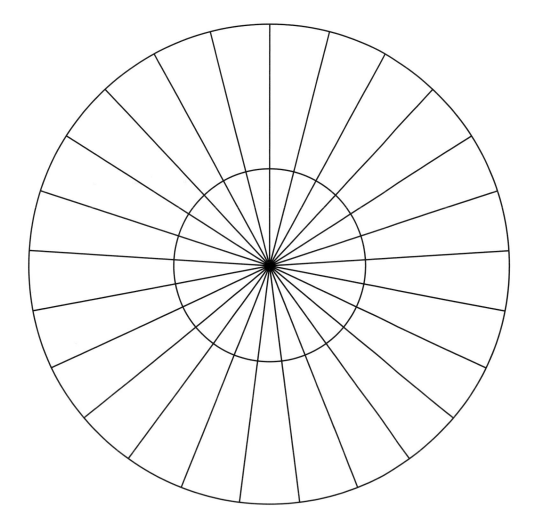

TEMPLATES

ACKNOWLEDGMENTS

Thank you to the team at Storey, who faced unprecedented challenges in the process of producing this book. Like the best engineers, they worked the problem to make it happen. And a special thank-you to Deanna, Nancy, Will, and Sarah for all your support and guidance along the way.

METRIC CONVERSION CHART

Weight

To convert	to	multiply
ounces	grams	ounces by 28.35

Length

To convert	to	multiply
inches	millimeters	inches by 25.4
inches	centimeters	inches by 2.54
feet	meters	feet by 0.3048
yards	meters	yards by 0.9144

Volume

To convert	to	multiply
pints	milliliters	pints by 473.18
pints	liters	pints by 0.473
quarts	milliliters	quarts by 946.36
quarts	liters	quarts by 0.946

INDEX

PLAY, CREATE, AND EXPERIMENT
with More Books from Storey

by Margaret Larson

Learn key skills like how to drive a nail and operate a power drill. Then use what you've learned to build 17 fun and creative projects including your very own workbench, a clever portable tic-tac-toe game, a message board, and more.

by Norma Jean Haynes, Ann Sayre Wiseman & John Langstaff

Music is inside everyone! With this playful guide, you'll tap out your own rhythm, compose, perform, and record your own melodies — and even craft your own instruments, from flowerpot chimes to a milk carton guitar.

by Jonathan Adolph

From water fireworks and soda stalactites to a caterpillar hatchery, a balloon barometer, and much more, you can conduct these 40 fun, foolproof, and fascinating science experiments in a glass canning jar.